YOU'RE STRONGER THAN YOU THINK

YOU'RE STRONGER THAN YOU THINK

TAPPING INTO THE SECRETS OF
EMOTIONALLY RESILIENT PEOPLE

PETER UBEL, M.D.

McGraw·Hill

New York   Chicago   San Francisco   Lisbon   London   Madrid   Mexico City
Milan   New Delhi   San Juan   Seoul   Singapore   Sydney   Toronto

Library of Congress Cataloging-in-Publication Data

Ubel, Peter A.
 You're stronger than you think : tapping into the secrets of emotionally resilient
people / Peter Ubel.—1st ed.
  p. cm.
 ISBN 0-07-146480-8 (alk. paper)
 1. Resilience (Personality trait) I. Title.

BF698.35.R47U24 2006
155.2′4—dc22
                                                                2005030058

1 2 3 4 5 6 7 8 9 0   FGR/FGR   0 9 8 7 6

ISBN 0-07-146480-8

McGraw-Hill books are available at special quantity discounts to use as premiums and
sales promotions, or for use in corporate training programs. For more information, please
write to the Director of Special Sales, Professional Publishing, McGraw-Hill, Two Penn
Plaza, New York, NY 10121-2298. Or contact your local bookstore.

This book is printed on acid-free paper.

To Sarah Lezotte, Jay and M. B. Schreiner,
Andy Crawford (I miss you!), Alex Crawford, Greg and
Ruth Hughes, Scott Mackler, Lynn Snyder-Mackler,
and all the other Snyder-Macklers—I can't thank you
enough for all that you have taught me.
I dedicate this book to you.

Contents

Acknowledgments

This book began a half dozen years ago on a trip to Palo Alto, California, where I visited my friend George Loewenstein who was on a sabbatical. At the time, I was conducting research on bioethics and economics, and one of the questions I was thinking through was the question of whose values ought to be incorporated into cost effectiveness analyses (an economic measure commonly used in health care). I won't bore you with the details of this question. Suffice it to say that most health economists believe that if you want to assess how bad it is to have any given illness, you should not ask patients with the illness but should describe the illness to the general public and ask them to imagine how bad it would be. This practice is controversial, of course. Healthy people frequently overestimate how bad they would feel if they had health problems. So that day in Palo Alto, George and I decided to figure out why the general public imagines most illnesses to be far worse than people with those illnesses report the same illnesses to be. We started conducting research studies, exploring whether people with illnesses are really as happy as they say they are and whether healthy people are able to accurately imagine what it's like to have illness or disability. In the process, I became fascinated with emotional resilience, and this book was the result. I thank George for helping me begin working in this fascinating area.

In the process of conducting my research, I have been fortunate to work with many great people. While at the University of Pennsylvania, I worked with David Asch, Jon Baron, Jack Hershey, and Chris Jepson, and I owe them a debt of gratitude that goes beyond the issues I explore in this book. At the University of Michigan, I have been able to work with people like Norbert Schwarz, Stephanie Brown, Jason Riis, Angie Fagerlin, Laura Damschroder, Brian Zikmund-Fisher, and Heather Pond Lacey. But by far the closest colleague I've worked with in Michigan on the issues I explore in this book has been Dylan Smith, who has patiently waited for me to start getting a clue about the wonders of social psychology, his chosen profession.

I had lots of help writing and rewriting this book. At the research center that I direct, I have been able to work with a marvelous group of University of Michigan students, many of whom have had a role in typing and editing my manuscript. For example, I mistakenly called Christopher Reeve "Christopher Reeves," perhaps thinking of the actor who had played Superman on that old TV show. Thankfully one of my students picked up on that mistake. I thank all of these students, Shanen Beck, Jim Dunn, Andy Englehart, Susan Fenn, Megan Richards, Melissa Shauver, Sandra Serna Smith, and give special thanks to Veronica Uzarski who in the midst of working more than eighty hours a week at school and another job still managed to come to our center with her sense of humor and energy intact. I've also benefited from wonderful administrative assistance from Heidi Kutzley and Barbara Turgyan.

A number of people read and commented on various chapters in this book, including some of the people already mentioned. But in addition I thank Maria Silviera, Atul Gawande, Jim Boyle, Phil Pochoda, and Danny Levitas for helpful advice. And I cannot thank Michele Heisler enough for managing to slog through the entire book, some parts more than once, and managing to both encourage me in my writing while providing me with much needed and greatly appreciated constructive criticism.

John Aherne at McGraw-Hill also read through the whole book, but that was his job so it is hard to thank him for that. But he has gone well beyond his job, helping to find ways to promote this book and encouraging me about the possibilities of helping this book reach a broad audience. For that I am extremely grateful.

I am enormously indebted to my agent, Rob McQuilkin, who discovered my book proposal lying at the bottom of a pile of papers and was able to imagine that I had some potential as a writer. I simply cannot imagine working with a better agent, and I hope that we are able to work together on many more books.

The Beginning of the Struggle

Greg Hughes woke up and got out of bed, and before he even had a chance to drag a comb across his head, a sharp pain grabbed hold of his right leg. Greg had been experiencing intermittent muscle cramps in that leg for a couple of weeks, but, not being a big exerciser, the cramps were little more than a nuisance. He did not feel the cramps when repairing cars down at Northwest Tire and Service Station or when walking his two dogs. But that morning, his leg cramps were unusually intense, strong enough to double him over in pain.

Leaning over to rub his leg, Greg was gripped by severe chest pains, tightness actually, as if someone was wringing out his sternum like a sponge. Thinking he was having a heart attack, he took two aspirins and asked his wife, Ruth, to call 911. The paramedics arrived a few minutes later, and Greg told them his chest pain had gone away. Trained to be cautious, the paramedics insisted on transporting him to the hospital anyway. That was fine by Greg, whose right leg pain was getting worse, like someone was inflating a balloon under the skin of his thigh, each pump of the balloon coinciding with his heart beat. Greg's pain was so intense that the paramedics called the hospital for permission to give him a dose of morphine in the ambulance. They received permission, but the morphine did nothing to relieve his pain.

The paramedics raced Greg from his home in Dansville—a farming community in south central Michigan with a population of 2,800 people—to the nearest community hospital and wheeled him into the emergency room, where he rolled past four patients separated from each other by nothing but a series of flimsy hospital curtains. Greg did not see any doctors attending to the other patients, and now he lay on his cot, without a doctor in sight and with leg pain so severe it felt like he had just stumbled upon a land mine. He cursed at the emergency room staff, complaining that he needed to see a doctor right away, but they had lost all sense of urgency since his chest pain had gone away. A few minutes later, his mother showed up so Greg immediately stopped cursing. But the pain continued to increase and soon he was at it again. "I need a goddamn doctor now!" he shouted. A physician showed up and gave him a second shot of morphine; Greg blacked out.

He wouldn't regain consciousness for three-and-a-half weeks.

A Long Three-and-a-Half Weeks

During the time of Greg's coma, Ruth was almost constantly by his side, while an endless stream of doctors tried to figure out what was wrong with his leg. Thinking back on those horrible days, Ruth remembers an overwhelming blur of fatigue, confusion, and desperation. Sometime during that first day, Greg's right leg turned black. The doctors told her that Greg's leg was not getting enough blood, but they had not discovered why. Desperate to save his leg, they cut into Greg's groin and tried to figure out what was going on with his right femoral artery, the main vessel supplying blood to his leg. The artery looked fine, so they stitched his groin back together. During the next day or so, as Ruth remembers events, Greg's left leg became purple and mottled, as if he had stepped outside on a cold winter day without any pants on. The doctors ordered an emergency CAT scan, which showed what appeared to be a clot in his abdominal aorta, the artery that feeds blood to the right and left femoral arteries. They needed to do something about the clot right away, but Greg was too sick to survive any treatment. The lack of blood flow to his right leg had made it susceptible to gangrene, which, in turn, had seeded his blood with bacteria. Greg was septic and in shock.

The bacteria caused Greg's blood pressure to plummet and his kidneys to stop working. At this point, Greg's doctors realized that his only hope for survival was to fly in an air ambulance to the University of Michigan Hospital, concerned that the hour-long ride in a ground ambulance would be more than Greg could survive. The flight team arrived fifteen minutes later and whisked Greg into a helicopter. Shortly after liftoff, Greg's heart stopped and the flight nurses jump-started it with a jolt of electricity. It was the first of four times his heart would stop that day.

Upon arriving at the university hospital, Greg was met by a team of vascular surgeons who discovered that Greg had experienced an aortic dissection. The aorta is a large artery that rises up from the heart and loops down in the back of the chest and abdomen, from which arteries to the brain, arms, and internal organs branch out. Somewhere below the kidneys, the aorta splits in two, to direct blood into the legs through the right and left femoral arteries. Greg's aorta was not sending blood to either leg because a false channel, a dissection, had developed between the layers of his aorta. Greg's blood was slamming into a dead end between the inner and outer layers of his aorta's wall.

In the weeks after I met Greg, I would be reminded of his aortic dissection each time I slipped on my favorite old winter jacket. The lining was falling apart, with a tear in the seam connecting the lining to the shoulder of my jacket, causing me on more than one occasion to lose my arm in the false passage between the inner and outer linings. My hand would slam into the end of my coat lining the same way Greg's blood was slamming into the dead-end channel within his abdominal aorta. In my case, I simply needed to remove my arm and reinsert it, more carefully, into the true opening. In Greg's case, the solution wasn't so simple. As his blood slammed into the false opening, it clotted, creating a blockage so large that it pushed on the inside wall of Greg's abdominal aorta, closing off the true path so that Greg's blood no longer had a way to get to his legs.

Once the surgeons figured out that Greg had an aortic dissection, they quickly wheeled him into an operating room, where they repaired his aorta with a foot of grafting material. But, unfortunately, over the course of seven more operations, the surgeons were forced to amputate both of Greg's legs, approximately six inches below his groin. Greg's life was saved, but his legs were lost.

When Greg woke up from his coma two-and-a-half weeks later, he found himself lying in an intensive care unit bed. Somehow, as he came to grips with his strange surroundings, he knew that his legs were gone, even though he was too weak and confused to confirm his suspicions. He remembers gesturing toward them and seeing Ruth nod that yes, his legs were gone. He remembers fading in and out of consciousness for a few days and, when all seemed lost, remembers his dead grandfather appearing to him in a dream, urging him to fight for his life. One day, with Ruth seated at his bedside, Greg hallucinated that a panther was standing on her left side and a lion on her right. He remembers the confused look on her face when he reached out to pet the imaginary animals.

Not very many healthy forty-five-year-olds wake up one morning and lose their legs. Most people with leg amputations have chronic diseases, such as diabetes, that slowly block the blood supply to their legs. They bump their foot on something one day and get a small wound. But the wound does not heal because it is not receiving enough blood, so over days or weeks the wound becomes infected. After a long struggle, and despite the help of antibiotics and pain medications, they learn that nothing will relieve their pain or cure their infection other than an amputation. For these people, an amputation is the culmination of a slow, chronic event. For many, in fact, the amputation is a relief.

But Greg's aortic dissection came out of nowhere. He had no time to emotionally prepare for a life without legs. Nor could he console himself with the thought that the amputations had relieved him of chronic pain and misery. Instead, without any warning, Greg's life had irreversibly changed. He would never work as an auto mechanic again—without legs, he would be unable to lean over and peer into a car engine. Hunting in the woods and walking around the corner to the Wooden Nickel Pub—all these things that he used to take for granted—were now part of his past.

What would it be like to wake up one morning and lose your legs, your job, and your favorite hobbies? When asked to imagine such a predicament, most people cannot fathom finding happiness again. Many say they would rather die than live without legs. What about Greg then? What kind of life can he expect? Will he be able to find happiness?

The Hedonic Treadmill

In the 1970s, a trio of psychologists led by Philip Brickman measured the happiness of three groups of people: (1) *lottery winners* who had won as much as one million dollars within the past year (the equivalent of tens of millions of today's dollars); (2) *motor vehicle accident victims* who were now living with either paraplegia or quadriplegia; and (3) *control subjects*, regular Joes and Josephines from the same neighborhoods as the other two groups. Not surprisingly, the lottery winners were happier than the control subjects who, in turn, were happier than the accident victims. But to almost everyone's surprise, the happiness of these three groups didn't differ by very much. The fabulously wealthy lottery winners were barely, almost imperceptibly, happier than the regular Joes and Josephines who, in turn, weren't all that much happier than the accident victims. Brickman called this phenomenon a *hedonic treadmill*, a metaphor capturing the idea that when people's circumstances change, their emotions stay in pretty much the same place, like a person running on a treadmill, who, despite the pumping of his legs, never really changes location.

Other psychologists refer to this phenomenon as *emotional adaptation*, a metaphor created to conjure up images of the way people physiologically adapt to changing environments. For example, when people walk from the bright sun into a dark room, it is difficult to see for a while. But their central nervous systems quickly respond, causing their pupils to dilate so they can adapt to their new surroundings. Human bodies adapt to cold and hot temperatures in a similar way. A 55°F afternoon in September feels chilly because people's bodies have adapted to summer temperatures, whereas a 55°F day in March is an excuse to walk outside in a pair of shorts. The metaphor of emotional adaptation is intended to suggest that, just as people's vision returns toward normal once they adapt to a change in ambient light, so too will their emotions return to normal once they adapt to their new circumstances.

Are People as Happy as They Say They Are?

I first met Greg Hughes in the University of Michigan Rehabilitation Hospital, where he had been transferred after he awoke from his coma. To gain insight into the obstacles people face when they experience new disabilities, I had been touring the hospital with Dr. James Leonard, chairman of the Medical School's Physical Medicine and Rehabilitation Department. While there, I met a teenage boy who had lost an arm in a silo accident, several people who had experienced new spinal cord injuries, and a few elderly patients who had undergone amputations because of vascular disease and diabetes.

But Greg stood out from the crowd because his burly, powerful physique was hard to reconcile with his near death in intensive care three weeks earlier. He also stood out because he was relatively gregarious compared to many other patients in the rehabilitation hospital who looked embarrassed or shocked about their new disabilities. But more than anything, Greg stood out because of his attitude. Despite having lost his legs so recently, Greg was upbeat and optimistic, describing his amputations as a "minor setback." He even joked about the disappearance of his legs, which the hospital had incinerated, razzing the surgeons about his missing parts. "When I fix people's cars," he told them, "I give them their money back if I can't show them the broken parts. Any chance you guys will give me my money back?!"

Visiting Greg in the hospital, I couldn't tell whether he'd truly adapted to his situation or was simply in denial. Greg had witnessed what disability could do to a person's life. Several decades earlier, his uncle had experienced a severely disabling car accident and, unlike most of the people in Brickman's study, did not recover emotionally from his disabilities. He drank too much alcohol and his marriage fell apart, famously so in fact—his wife snuck into the bedroom one night while he lay in a drunken stupor, poured gasoline around him, and lit a match, burning him to death. As portrayed in *Burning Bed*, a Farrah Fawcett movie from the 1980s, Greg's uncle was a wife-beater. Greg disputes this characterization, saying that his uncle was too disabled to physically abuse anyone. But Greg readily acknowledges that his uncle's life was ruined by his disability.

Could Greg be projecting a happy demeanor to convince himself he wouldn't end up like his uncle? Indeed, how do we ever know when someone else is truly happy?

Measuring Happiness

For the past five years, I have been working with a team of social scientists and clinicians to figure out whether people with chronic illness or disability are as resilient as they often report being. Since the time of Brickman's lottery winner study, experts have questioned whether people's emotions are really as immune to circumstance as that study suggested. To come to my own answer, I pored through the literature to learn how social scientists measure people's happiness. You might need to sit down for this next bit because it is pretty technical—I have found that the most common method social scientists use to measure people's happiness is to ask people how happy they are, using such questions as "How satisfied are you with your overall life?" or "What percentage of the time are you happy?"

At first glance, this method is not very convincing. People may not want to admit that they are unhappy when researchers ask them. And even if they try their best to answer researchers' questions honestly, their answers might be influenced by forces beyond their awareness. For example, people actually report greater overall life satisfaction on sunny days than rainy ones. The weather influences people's momentary moods and these moods influence the way they think about their overall lives. That means that when you catch people on a rainy day, you will get an overly pessimistic view of how happy they usually are.

Indeed, my colleague Norbert Schwarz, a psychologist at the University of Michigan, once conducted a study where he surreptitiously arranged for a random sample of research participants to find a dime on a photocopy machine before filling out a questionnaire. The questionnaire asked them about their overall happiness in life, and those participants who had found a dime reported exaggeratedly high levels of overall happiness. Buoyed by finding the dime, they overstated how good their lives were. Those who hadn't found a dime were less exuberant.

Weather and dimes aside, researchers have assessed survey questions about happiness by conducting what are known as validation tests and found that they usually do a pretty good job of measuring true happiness. For example, researchers have found that people's answers to questions about how happy they are correspond well with their facial expressions. When people pretend to be happy, they smile with their mouths but not with the rest of their faces. But when they are truly happy, their eyes move in accordance with their mouths in a predictable and reproducible manner called a Duchenne's smile (named after the great nineteenth-century physician Guillaume Duchenne, whose name is also linked with the most famous form of muscular dystrophy). Researchers have confirmed the diagnosticity of Duchenne's smiles by inducing happy moods in people and analyzing their facial expressions. To do so, they asked people how happy they were and then surreptitiously observed them. They found that people who report being happy are more likely to exhibit these Duchenne's smiles.

When Greg Hughes said he was as happy as ever, then, should I have believed him? If a man tells me he weighs 160 pounds and his wife says he weighs 180 pounds, I can place him on a scale and see if he is reporting his weight accurately. But if a man tells me he is happy, how do I know that's true? I cannot simply put him on a happiness scale and find out the truth: "Hmm, it looks like you're a 7 today; better get back on that happiness diet." There was no simple, irrefutable way for me to validate Greg's self-reported happiness. I needed to dig deeper, to figure out just what it means for someone to confront adversity and believe that they were made stronger because of the struggle. I needed to uncover the secrets of people's emotional resilience.

Responding to Adversity

In a decade and a half of practicing primary care medicine, I have encountered thousands of people who have experienced serious adversity. I currently take care of patients at the Ann Arbor Veterans Affairs Hospital, where a typical patient might have hypertension, diabetes, emphysema, hearing loss, impotence, a touch of heart failure, or chronic pain from a wartime wound. Working with these patients has given me insight into the way people respond to adversity. I have learned that many are amazingly resilient, responding to adversity with optimism and determination.

I have also learned, however, that such resilience is neither effortless nor automatic. In fact, many struggle because of adversity, and some are overwhelmed and made bitter by that struggle. Not everyone can emotionally cope with difficult circumstances. Suicide rates among people with spinal cord injuries, for example, are more than seven times greater than among the general population. And even when people are able to find happiness, this is a struggle that can take many years.

Emotional resilience is a well-kept secret. Most of us significantly underestimate our ability to overcome adversity. In the chapters that follow, I will discuss some of the secrets of emotional resilience. I will show that people often respond to adversity in surprising ways, overcoming huge struggles relatively easily while tripping up on seemingly smaller obstacles. I will describe the specific struggles facing people such as Greg Hughes.

We can learn from their struggles—learn to recognize and draw upon our own emotional resilience and learn how to improve the way we live our lives. Adversity often makes people stronger, focusing them on important life goals that they would otherwise be too busy or distracted to pursue. And learning from these struggles, we can improve our lives, even those of us who have not yet had to contend with serious adversity.

2

The Limits of the Imagination

Sarah Lezotte's kidney problems started in 1991 with what felt like a case of the flu. Fifty-eight years old at the time, she had never experienced any major health problems before, but these flu symptoms were lasting longer than normal. So Sarah decided to see her primary care doctor, who discovered that she had early signs of kidney failure. He referred her to a kidney specialist, who drew a slew of blood tests, ordered a pile of x-rays and ultrasounds, and finally biopsied her kidneys. Then he sat Sarah down and told Sarah her diagnosis: she had vasculitis, a generic term for inflammation (*itis*) of the blood vessels (*vasc*). Many diseases cause vasculitis, the best known being lupus. But Sarah did not have any of the diseases that typically cause vasculitis—she didn't have lupus or Sjögrens syndrome or polyarteritis nodosa. She didn't have scleroderma or sarcoidosis or giant cell arteritis. Instead, she was stuck with the vaguest of all diagnoses—plain old vasculitis—as if she had cancer but no one could tell her what kind of cancer: "Lung cancer? Breast cancer? Colon cancer?" the patient asks. "No," the doctor replies, "just cancer."

Without a more specific diagnosis, Sarah was stuck with some rather nonspecific treatments, such as prednisone, which puffed her face up like the Pillsbury doughboy, and Imuran, a chemotherapy drug that made her feel ninety years old. She dutifully took her pills every day, but her vasculitis continued to wreak havoc with her kidneys. Within three years, Sarah Lezotte began receiving dialysis.

Dreading Dialysis

What would it feel like to have kidney failure and be forced to undergo dialysis to stay alive? To be hooked up to a dialysis machine three times a week? Never to be able to eat fruits and vegetables without worrying that you will experience dangerous levels of potassium in your blood? To fear that drinking more than forty-eight ounces of liquid in a day will make you swell up like the Michelin man?

I have yet to take care of a patient who looked forward to the initiation of dialysis, no matter how severe their symptoms from failing kidneys. Prior to requiring dialysis, most experience years of progressive kidney failure. They watch their blood pressure and take their medicines in hopes of delaying the need for dialysis. Most recognize that dialysis will dramatically change their lives, forcing them to squeeze fifteen hours of treatment time into their weekly schedules and to forgo travel unless they can find dialysis centers willing to accommodate them. In imagining life on dialysis, their minds are usually filled with images of plastic tubing, impersonal machines, and, worst of all, needles.

People with progressive kidney failure are not alone in assuming that life on dialysis must be dismal. When my research team asked healthy people to imagine that they had end-stage kidney failure, they predicted that such an illness would leave them unhappy for the majority of their waking hours. Many told us they would give up more than half of their remaining life span to avoid becoming a dialysis patient. A significant number said they would rather be dead.

About the only group of people who think life on dialysis is not miserable are those actually *on* dialysis. When my team asked dialysis patients to estimate the percentage of time they were in good, neutral, or bad moods, they told us they were in good moods a majority of the time and in bad moods less than 20 percent of the time. In fact, their self-reported mood estimates were indistinguishable from those of a group of healthy people we interviewed (matched to the patients by age, gender, race, and education level). In other words, based on the self-reports, dialysis patients were just as happy as healthy people.

Waste products coursing through their veins, a banana cream pie away from a life-threatening potassium level, and they were as happy as healthy people? It is easy to question these glowing reports of life on dialysis given what we have learned about how people's global mood estimates are skewed by finding a dime on a copy machine. In fact, we had paid dialysis patients to tell us about their moods. Could receiving money from pleasant research assistants in itself make people happy, thereby causing them to overstate how happy they are?

Global Happiness Reports Versus Actual Moment-to-Moment Mood

The campus recruitment ad for Daniel Kahneman's study might have stated something like this: "Make money by experiencing pain!" The advertisement might have gone on to explain that students would be asked to place one hand into a bucket of freezing cold ice water for a period of time; then they would place their other hand into another bucket of ice water. Finally, they would be asked to choose one hand to place back into the ice bucket for a third session of pain, after which they would receive their payment.

The advertisement would not have said that students would place one hand into a bucket of ice water at 57°F for sixty seconds, an immersion that causes considerable pain for the entire minute. They would place the other hand into another bucket, also chilled to 57°F for sixty seconds, but then warmed to 59°F for thirty more seconds. Although 59°F is slightly warmer than 57°F, it is still quite painful. The students would not be told how long either hand had been in either bucket nor would they be informed of the temperature of either bucket. The experimenters were also careful to randomize which bucket was experienced first, the sixty-second or the ninety-second bucket, and which hand, their right or left, went into which bucket.

At this point in the experiment, Kahneman—a psychologist and Nobel laureate—asked students to choose which bucket to place their hand into for their third session. To minimize their pain, students would have been wise to choose the sixty-second bucket. After all, both buckets were equally painful for the first sixty seconds. The ninety-second bucket simply added thirty seconds of pain. Nevertheless, two-thirds of the students chose to repeat the longer, more painful immersion. (The researchers spared everyone the third experience, since their goal was to find out which experience people would decide is better to repeat.) Unaware of the temperature and duration of their first two cold-water immersions, most students perceived that the ninety-second immersion was less painful than the sixty-second one.

How could adding thirty seconds of pain to an experience make people perceive that the experience is less painful? People are notoriously bad at summing up the quality of their experiences over time. Consequently, when reflecting on the two ice buckets, students had a hard time figuring out which immersion lasted longer, but they distinctly remembered that one of the buckets got less painful over time, so they assumed that that bucket must have caused them less pain.

A similar phenomenon contributes to patients' memories of receiving a colonoscopy, a medical procedure in which a fiber-optic scope is inserted into a person's rectum to view their colon. Colonoscopies are rather uncomfortable with doctors pushing air into people's colons to look for polyps, uncomfortable enough that it is music to most patients' ears when the doctor says, "Okay, we're coming out now." But Kahneman and colleagues showed that people perceive this procedure to be less painful when the doctors keep the colonoscope inside for a little longer after the examination is complete, while reducing how much air they pump into the colon. Prolonging people's discomfort with a relatively good ending causes people to perceive experiences as less unpleasant overall.

Pleasure and pain are not remembered the same way they are experienced. People's memories are disproportionately influenced by peak experiences and by whether their experiences have good or bad endings. The duration of most experiences often plays a surprisingly small role in people's memories. As a result of these faulty rememberings, researchers are increasingly relying on novel ways of capturing people's true moment-to-moment experiences. In fact, my research team was skeptical enough of the happiness reports we received from dialysis patients that we sent each one home with a shiny new personal digital assistant (PDA) to find out how happy they really were. The PDAs were used to collect mood data over the course of one week.

We programmed the PDAs to beep at random intervals every ninety minutes or so for a week (during waking hours) to ask people about their moods. "Thinking back to right before this PDA beeped, what was your mood? How happy were you? How anxious, depressed, frustrated, joyful?" We gave PDAs to the same two groups I described earlier, the dialysis patients and the healthy controls who had reported happiness levels practically identical to each other. By collecting such data over the course of a week—out of the presence of our mood-elevating research assistants and including those early morning or late night hours when people might be emotionally overwhelmed by their health problems—we could find out whether people were as happy moment to moment as they told us they were overall.

Sarah Lezotte was one of the dialysis patients who participated in our PDA study. To learn more about how her kidney problems affected her life, I visited her several months after the study in her rural Michigan home. Sarah is a tiny, energetic woman, with short brown hair that doesn't look gussied up and a quick smile that doesn't look forced. Despite her diminutive size, she does not look as frail as you would expect from someone who has struggled with kidney disease for more than a decade.

She told me that when she first developed kidney problems in the early 1990s, she chose to receive peritoneal dialysis (PD), a form of treatment in which her own body was turned into a dialysis machine. To do this, a surgeon implanted a tube into Sarah's abdominal wall. The inside of the tube nestled underneath her skin but above her peritoneal membrane, a layer of connective tissue that separates her intestines from the lower layers of fat underneath her skin. Sarah's peritoneal membrane acted like a sieve. She would pour one-and-a-half liters of fluid through the tube, which would settle in underneath her skin but above her peritoneum. Waste products in Sarah's bloodstream would drift into her peritoneal space and bump into the dialysis fluid hanging out there. The dialysis fluid would equilibrate with waste products from her bloodstream, thereby drawing waste products out of her bloodstream. Four hours later, Sarah would drain the dialysis fluid and all the waste products within it and then pour in another one-and-a-half liters of clean dialysis liquid, starting the process all over again. She went through this process four times a day, with each filling and draining taking up another hour, leaving her a few hours of wiggle room to get in all four treatments within a twenty-four-hour period. Then she would wake up the next morning and start all over again.

"It was hard for me to be very active when I was on PD," Sarah told me. "With all that fluid inside me, I felt half pregnant all the time, and the pressure on my stomach gave me pretty bad heartburn most of the time. When you're on PD," she continued, "you have to slice your life up into four-hour intervals, because that's how long you have until you need to exchange the PD fluid. So, you can go out to dinner *or* you can go out to a movie, but you can't go out to dinner and a movie." Sarah described her PD life to me almost matter of factly, with no sense of bitterness.

Sarah remained on PD for about two years and remembers feeling like her life had settled into a relatively manageable routine. She got used to the constant bloated feeling and the almost constant heartburn. And she quickly adapted to the four-hour rhythms of her new life. But she did not exactly enjoy having kidney failure and hoped her health would remain good enough to receive a kidney transplant some day. She got the go-ahead for a transplant in 1996, when her doctors discovered that one of her nine children, Anne, was a good match to be a kidney donor. "Anne's donation was uncomplicated, thank God, but my operation was a total mess. The kidney never really 'took.' I'm not sure what went wrong, but instead of waking up in a normal hospital bed, I woke up in the intensive care unit. I don't remember a lot about my time there, but eventually I was transferred out of intensive care, and my new kidney began working well enough that they could take me off of dialysis. I was very happy, but I still felt really sick. They said my creatinine [a waste product that can indicate improper levels of kidney functions] was still high."

The doctors said it was only a matter of time before she would need to go back on dialysis. For the next three years, Sarah enjoyed her life off of dialysis, ever mindful of the likelihood that her daughter's kidney, tucked away in Sarah's belly not too far from where her daughter's life had begun, would die.

Kidney failure is often a subtle, progressive process, with people's health shifting imperceptibly as their kidneys slow down. In healthy people, creatinine levels generally hover around 1. Take away one kidney, and most people's creatinine levels will still remain around 1, because the remaining kidney is generally strong enough to clear all of the waste products on its own. (That is why it was possible for Sarah's daughter to donate one of her kidneys.) If people's creatinine levels rise from 1 to 2, that usually means the kidneys are doing only half of their job, with waste levels double what they should be. This doubling of waste levels sounds awful, but people with this level of kidney function are almost never symptomatic. In fact, most people do not require dialysis until their creatinine levels double one or two more times.

For a while, Sarah's creatinine level hovered in the 3 to 4 range, but after her new kidney was damaged by the antibiotics she needed to take to try and keep the kidney healthy, the creatinine slowly started climbing. At that point, her eventual need for dialysis was obvious. Under normal circumstances, her doctors would have watched her closely until the time was right for her to start back on dialysis. But Sarah never seems to experience normal circumstances. Instead, two years after her transplant, Sarah began to lose weight and her tongue turned white, signs of a fungal infection probably caused by all the antirejection drugs she was taking. It took a while for her doctors to get the infection under control. Until then, every time she had a spoonful of applesauce or a slice of bread, it felt like she was swallowing gravel. Sarah continued to lose weight, and her white blood cell count rose, causing her doctors to conclude that she had an intestinal infection. They blasted her with an antibiotic called gentamycin, which cured her infection but tragically also damaged her new kidney. It was time to go back on dialysis.

As if things weren't bad enough, two weeks after going back on dialysis, Sarah experienced a bowel perforation. She is not sure why her intestine decided to spring a leak, but there she was, back in intensive care, with a twelve-inch surgical scar running down her abdomen and, of all things, a colostomy bag protruding from her abdomen.

Ask people to imagine being a dialysis patient and most predict they will be miserable. They feel the same way about living with a colostomy, a plastic pouch that protrudes from the abdominal wall for people who cannot have bowel movements. Put the two together—dialysis plus a colostomy—and many people say they would rather be dead than live with such terrible health problems. Sarah describes how she felt at the time: "I spent a horrible month recovering in the hospital. When I got home, things weren't much better. I had to drive to a dialysis center three times a week. And the colostomy was very difficult for me at first. I couldn't change the bag myself, so my husband was nice enough to do that for me. He was really good about that, although I can't say the experience made him find me particularly sexy. I didn't know whether I could go on living like this much longer. Everything seemed to be falling apart on me. I got so depressed that I thought about going off dialysis, and I even asked my doctor how long I would survive if I stopped dialysis treatments. He said I wouldn't live more than a couple of weeks but urged me not to quit dialysis yet. I decided to stick it out until my new grandchild arrived."

Sarah's second daughter was pregnant with her first child, and having this occasion to look forward to gave Sarah the will to live a little longer. Meanwhile, she began regaining some of the strength that she had lost during her long hospital stay. Sarah was an exercise instructor before she got sick, so she decided to start a program for herself. She also got the cataracts removed from her eyes that had prevented her from reading all the books that were stacked up on her shelves. Eventually, she found that her mood began to improve, and she no longer contemplated going off dialysis. Then, one year later, Sarah returned to the hospital in order to get her colostomy reversed.

If you had met Sarah for the first time then, perhaps walking into the dialysis center, you might have felt sorry for her having to suffer with kidney failure and more. But Sarah's perspective was different. "My *only* problem was kidney disease. I didn't have a colostomy anymore!"

So what was Sarah's life like as a dialysis patient? When we asked her to estimate her typical mood, Sarah, like most of the dialysis patients in our study, told us she was in a good mood the majority of her waking hours. In her case, given how much sicker she had been in the past, such an answer might be plausible. But Sarah's story reminds us of an important consideration in imagining the lives of people with kidney failure—most have many health problems beyond simple kidney failure. Like Sarah, some have vasculitis, which can affect other body parts. More commonly, people develop kidney failure after years of diabetes or high blood pressure. Consequently, many experience not only kidney failure but also a host of other medical problems, most commonly heart disease, vision loss, and damage to their feet and legs from hardening of the arteries. Most of the dialysis patients in our study, who told us they were so happy, had many other health problems to cope with besides kidney failure. Could they really be as happy as they said? It was time to find out what their PDAs had to say about their moods.

When we downloaded data from the PDAs, we discovered, just as we feared, that dialysis patients had overestimated how often they were in extremely good moods. Rather than experiencing really good moods 40 percent of the time, as they had told our research assistants, they experienced such moods only 20 percent of the time.

I don't believe these dialysis patients were lying to our research assistants to cover up how miserable they were. Instead, when they estimated what their moods were like in a typical week, they probably thought back over the previous week, and the extremely good moods they had experienced came to mind more easily than the mildly positive moods they had experienced.

Science is fun when you develop a theory to explain a phenomenon and can test whether that theory fits with other phenomena. For example, if the memorability of extreme moods accounts for these overestimations, then the dialysis patients should also overestimate the percent of the time they spend in really *bad* moods—which is exactly what we found. They predicted being in extremely bad moods 6 percent of the time, while experiencing such moods only 1 percent of the time—a result that also punctures the theory that dialysis patients overstated their good moods because they couldn't acknowledge how unhappy they were. Continuing this line of reasoning, we figured that if the memorability of extreme moods accounts for these overestimations, healthy people should *also* overestimate the percentage of time they spend in really good and really bad moods. Which, again, is exactly what we found. People—whether healthy or sick—predicted they would experience extremely good and bad moods a smaller proportion of the time than they *actually* experienced such moods.

The PDA method was proving to be a nice way to compare people's actual moods to the moods they predicted, revealing that people do not have perfect insight into their emotional lives.

So, what did the PDAs tell us about how happy these two groups of people were? Both groups had estimated that they were in good moods approximately two-thirds of the time, with some of their predicted moods being extremely good and some being only mildly pleasant. They had overestimated the frequency of the extremely good moods. But had they been wrong to say that they were in good moods the majority of the time?

No. Just as they had predicted, dialysis patients reported being in good moods approximately two-thirds of the time. In fact, they reported strikingly similar levels of happiness as healthy people, as well as similarly low levels of anxiety and depression. Based on their moment-to-moment moods then, dialysis patients were indistinguishable from healthy people.

It appears that when these dialysis patients told us they were happy the majority of the time, they knew what they were talking about.

Why Is It So Difficult to Imagine Dialysis Patients Being Happy?

Dialysis patients are generally happy, and yet few of them would have predicted that this could be the case. The general public imagines life on dialysis as being filled with unhappiness, and yet in our study the dialysis patients were just as happy as healthy people. Why is it so hard to imagine that these dialysis patients are happy?

When people imagine unfamiliar circumstances, they often focus their attention too narrowly on the unique aspects of these circumstances—the parts of their lives that would change—without considering the many ways their lives would be unaffected by the new circumstances. Psychologists call this phenomenon a *focusing illusion*. Imagine, for example, that you are a high school senior choosing between attending two similar universities, one in the upper Midwest and the other in Southern California. Where do you think you would be happier? If you are like most people, you would expect to be happier in California where you would be able to enjoy year-round sunshine. Yet when psychologists David Schkade and Daniel Kahneman measured the happiness of college students in California and the Midwest, they found no difference. Both groups of students were equally happy.

When comparing college life in California and the Midwest, most students focus their thoughts on an obvious difference between the two locations—the weather—ignoring all the other parts of college life that would influence their moods. Imagining life in California, midwesterners envision beach parties and scantily clad classmates. Thinking about life in the Midwest, Californians imagine flat landscapes and parka-clad coeds. Yet, most of college life has nothing to do with bathing suits or parkas. Students enjoy football games and music recitals and suffer through organic chemistry labs and 8 A.M. exams, whether they live in California or the Midwest. In fact, weather does not affect people's moods as much as they anticipate, with good weather primarily creating positive moods only among those who spend the majority of their waking hours outdoors.

Focusing Illusions and Adversity

The same kind of focusing illusion that influences how college students think about California versus the Midwest also influences the way people think about illness and disability. When imagining paraplegia, for example, many people without paraplegia focus on what it would feel like to get around in a wheelchair or to lose the ability to enjoy favorite pastimes; they do not think about all those aspects of their lives that would be unaffected by paraplegia, such as their ability to enjoy a television show, a good conversation, or a delicious meal. When imagining dialysis, they focus on needles, blood-filled tubes, and 12 hours a week of being attached to a machine, ignoring the other 150 hours of the week when they would not be at the dialysis center. And they overlook the social companionship they are likely to experience at the dialysis center.

But are focusing illusions inevitable? Most experts don't think so. For example, psychologists Daniel Gilbert and Timothy Wilson have shown that college football fans overestimate how much the outcome of the game will influence their moods over the following week because the fans focus too narrowly on the game without thinking enough about all the intervening events that will affect their moods later in the week. Yet, these two researchers have also shown that this kind of focusing illusion can be avoided. When football fans fill out an imaginary diary describing the week they expect to experience following a football game, they think more broadly about all the events in a typical week, other than a football game, that would influence their moods. As a result, they no longer mistakenly predict how strongly the football game will affect their moods.

Can Defocusing Help?

Encouraged by these results, my colleagues and I set out to see if we could rid people of a focusing illusion when they imagined life with a disability. We tried to *defocus* people, to get them to think more broadly about how disabilities would affect their lives. Worried that people would focus too narrowly on how specific aspects of their lives that would be affected by experiencing paraplegia from a below-the-knee amputation, we asked them to think about how such disabilities would affect a broad range of life domains, such as their work, spiritual, and family lives. We theorized that these broader thought processes would make people realize that the disability in question would have little effect on their lives as a whole.

As expected, we found that many viewed these disabilities less negatively after thinking more broadly about their lives, commenting on how our defocusing exercise helped them think more thoroughly about what life with a disability would be like. But to our surprise, for every person who viewed life with a disability less negatively after our exercise, two or three others viewed the disability *more negatively*. For most, the more they thought about life with a disability, the worse they imagined it would be.

People overestimate the long-term emotional impact of illness and disability, imagining that kidney failure or a spinal cord injury will make them miserable, when, as we have seen, the majority of people with kidney failure and spinal cord injuries are happy. Indeed, there seems to be no easy way to get people to think more broadly (or accurately) about what life with such circumstances is really like.

As mentioned earlier, I met with Sarah Lezotte three months after she had participated in our PDA study in hopes of gaining some insight into how dialysis patients manage to find happiness despite having such poor health. What I didn't mention was that, by the time I met with Sarah, she was no longer a dialysis patient. Two months after completing our PDA study, she received another transplant, this time from an organ donor and not a relative. Her health was now better than it had been in more than a decade, and she was feeling more energetic and optimistic than she had in years. I was delighted about her good fortune, but I still wanted her perspective on how she had been able to find so much happiness during her long struggle with kidney failure. So I was surprised to learn now that she did not have very positive memories of her life on dialysis.

"Dialysis days were essentially lost," she told me. She explained that she would drive forty minutes to the dialysis center, remain there for three-plus hours on dialysis, and then drive forty minutes back home. By then, her morning would be gone and after a brief lunch, she would settle down for a nap, exhausted by the long commute and the tiring dialysis session. But the truly hard part was the wiped-out feeling she got after the session. Healthy kidneys filter people's blood twenty-four hours a day, seven days a week. Sarah was receiving dialysis three times a week, for about 3 hours at a shot, giving her 9 or 10 hours of dialysis time to make up for the 168 hours her kidneys would have normally been on the job during the week. If they had been working, Sarah's kidneys would have slowly adjusted her potassium levels and her fluid balance, while continuously excreting waste products, like urea. Instead, in between dialysis sessions, Sarah's potassium level would rise, her fluid and waste products would build up, and then the dialysis machine would pull it all out of her bloodstream, making her feel like she had been put through a car wash, inside out. No wonder Sarah was so exhausted after leaving the dialysis center.

Not that fatigue was a new experience for Sarah, who had been pregnant eleven times in fourteen years, giving birth to nine healthy children. Her husband, an electrician, worked long hours to support his large family, which meant each day Sarah busied herself making eleven breakfasts, lunches, and dinners; doing three loads of laundry; and completing an endless pile of other tasks. She had lived through nine years of waking up in the middle of the night to care for a new baby; thirteen years of nondisposable diapers to change; and, most difficult for me to imagine of all, fourteen years of having toddlers in the household without even one sippy cup. "You could say that I was well prepared for kidney failure," she quipped.

Conversely, Sarah described nondialysis days as being much better. Her mornings were not consumed by her dialysis sessions, and she was not thrown off keel by the sudden shift of fluids and electrolytes brought upon her by the dialysis machine. But even on nondialysis days, life was hardly normal. Because of her kidney failure, Sarah could not drink more than forty-eight ounces of liquid each day. More accurately, she was not *supposed* to drink more than that each day: "It seems like all the patients at the dialysis center are scolded once or twice a week for gaining too much water weight in between dialysis sessions. I mean, forty-eight ounces?" Given her druthers, Sarah would have sat in the backyard sipping iced tea and reading a good book, but forty-eight ounces was hardly enough to get her a couple chapters into a juicy novel.

Sarah had given me insight into how dialysis had affected the rhythm of her day-to-day life, but I still did not have a feel for how it had affected her overall mood. "Oh, I hated being on dialysis, it was miserable," she said.

Miserable? I was surprised she said that because I had her data. I knew that Sarah was happy during her dialysis days, or at least I knew that she said she was happy when she carried around our PDA. I reminded her that she reported being happy the majority of the time. "Yes, I believe you," she said. "But you see, unlike other dialysis patients, I had hope for receiving a transplant. I don't know if I would have been so happy if it hadn't been for that hope." She had told me earlier that she had received a transplant much faster than expected, waiting a few months instead of what was supposed to be a couple years. I asked her whether being on this lengthy transplant waiting list is really what made her happy. She couldn't say, but she expected that such hope was key to her happiness—a happiness, by the way, that she had largely forgotten about a few minutes earlier when describing her life on dialysis.

Intrigued by how unhappy she remembered being before her transplant, I revisited her description of the time in her life when she had the colostomy. She told me that if she had not been able to reverse the colostomy, she would have *never* found happiness again. Yet, even before reversing her colostomy, she had found the motivation to initiate an exercise program, hardly the actions of a woman who was emotionally succumbing to chronic illness. Once again, she said that hope was key to her emotional resilience. But hope for what? Was reversing her colostomy the key to her happiness? Sarah thought back on that time in her life: "I remember complaining once to my social worker, when I was really sick, telling her how hard things were. She told me 'the human spirit regenerates.' Maybe my spirit would have regenerated, I don't know."

Hindsight Isn't Always 20/20

As we've discussed, healthy people frequently underestimate how happy they would be if they experienced serious illness. But when I met with Sarah Lezotte, I witnessed another type of misperception: having been on and off dialysis for the previous ten years, she now seemed to have an overly negative view in retrospect of what it had been like to experience kidney failure. And so, rather than gaining insights about how she found happiness despite such a serious illness, I found instead that her instinct was to minimize just how happy she had been. With the success of her new transplant, Sarah was quite happy now. Indeed, after all she had gone through to complete the transplant, she assumed she must be much, much happier now than she had been before the transplant.

Sarah Lezotte is by no means unusual in being somewhat out of touch with her own emotional life. People are so convinced that happiness is a matter of circumstance that they forget how much they are actually able to adapt to their circumstances. I should have expected Sarah's memory to be tricked in this manner. We had already discovered in our PDA study that people have powerful intuitions about how severe illness ought to affect them, and that these intuitions shape the way they perceive their emotional lives. For example, we asked our dialysis patients to imagine what their moods would have been like if they had never experienced kidney disease. They predicted that they would live in an almost perpetual state of glee, a level of happiness significantly higher than the moods our healthy control subjects actually experienced. These overestimates occurred because people had trouble imagining that big changes in their lives would not have large emotional consequences.

Talking to Sarah, I was reminded of a study I had conducted in which my colleagues and I asked a group of dialysis patients, all of whom were waiting for kidney transplants, to predict what their lives would be like one year after receiving a successful transplant. Most transplant candidates were unemployed at the time we interviewed them and predicted they would have thriving careers if they received a kidney transplant. Most traveled out of town less than three or four nights a year because of the hassle of finding alternative dialysis sites. They predicted, on average, that after a successful transplant they would travel five to six *weeks* per year. In every domain we asked them about, transplant candidates predicted enormous improvements in their lives following a successful transplant. But people's lives did not improve half as much as they had predicted. Rather than travel six weeks per year, they traveled an average of six days. Rather than returning to full-time employment, most were lucky to have part-time jobs. People emotionally adapt to transplantation, just like they adapt to kidney failure.

In another quick example, my colleagues and I surveyed patients who had received colostomies at the University of Michigan over the past five years to find out about their happiness and quality of life. As it turns out, half the people we surveyed had subsequently been able to rid themselves of their colostomy through a second operation. Despite this improvement in their situations, these people were no happier than those who still had colostomies. Nevertheless, both groups imagined that having a colostomy would significantly affect their long-term moods. Those people who had previously experienced colostomies, in fact, remembered being miserable when they had their colostomies!

Misremembering, Misperceptions, and Mood

The phenomenon of misremembering how circumstances have affected our moods is not limited to people's beliefs about illness and disability. It happens in general life as well. For example, most adults have voted for, or at least taken sides, in many political elections in the course of their lives. And yet people have very little insight into how it will feel over the long run if their candidate loses the election. When George W. Bush ran against Ann Richards for governor of Texas, Richards's supporters predicted they would be miserable if Bush won. Yet, one month after the election, Richards's supporters were just as happy as they had been before the election, even growing to like Bush more than they had predicted. If people accurately remembered how they felt after previous elections, they wouldn't have overestimated the emotional impact of the Bush election. But people's memories cannot be trusted.

To give another, more mundane example, people often overestimate their preference for variety when shopping for groceries. They often select a variety of yogurts, assuming that they will be in strawberry moods one day and blueberry moods another, when in fact most yogurt lovers have a favorite flavor that they will prefer most days of the week. This phenomenon was clearly demonstrated in a clever study of Halloween trick-or-treaters conducted by the behavioral economists Daniel Read and George Loewenstein. Their research design was simple. They set themselves up in two houses next door to each other in a Pittsburgh neighborhood. When the trick-or-treaters came to Loewenstein's house first, he offered each of them two candy bars and recorded which candy bars each child chose, calling out data to me when the trick-or-treaters walked away: "The clown chose one Milky Way and one Snickers bar, and the kid with the *Friday the Thirteenth* hockey mask. . . ." In these cases, the kids typically chose two *different* candy bars, like the clown I described above. However, when the trick-or-treaters came to Read's house first, each house offered them only one candy bar. In these cases the children typically chose the same candy bar at each house.

To my mind, the most compelling evidence Loewenstein has collected demonstrating people's misestimates of their moods occurred at the Pittsburgh marathon. He was running in the race and, much like that Halloween night, hated to see a major event pass by without conducting a study. So, prior to the race, he asked people to say whether they had run a marathon before, what time they expected to finish in, and whether they would run an additional quarter mile at the end of the race for $10.00. He predicted that people would overestimate their willingness to run an extra quarter mile, even experienced marathon runners who ought to know better. But he did not predict his own mood very well. He did not foresee that when he finished the race, he would be too tired to collect his data. To my knowledge he has never completed this study!

I tell this marathon story in large part to make fun of Loewenstein, who is a good friend of mine (and a collaborator in the PDA study), but also to illustrate the universality of mispredictions and misestimations. Even people such as Loewenstein, who spend their lives studying people's emotional mispredictions, make the same kinds of mispredictions. Which puts Sarah Lezotte's misperceptions—about what her life had been like on dialysis—into perspective.

The Effect of Time

Is there anything we can do to improve the way people think about circumstances they might encounter? My research team has found that people's predictions about the emotional affects of illness and disability change when they are prompted to think about how their emotions are likely to change over time. We asked a group of people to imagine how happy they would be if they had paraplegia. Then we asked them to think about a terrible event that had occurred in their lives six or more months ago. Did their emotions get stronger or weaker over time? Did the event influence their long-term moods more or less than they would have guessed? Do they think the experience of paraplegia would get stronger or weaker over time? After a few such questions, we asked them once again to imagine how happy they would be if they experienced paraplegia. Their estimates changed dramatically—they predicted much more happiness than they had previously predicted after they had thought about their own recent mishaps. People do recognize that strong emotions generally fade over time. Ask them to imagine their moods one week, one month, and one year after experiencing a spinal cord injury, and they estimate dramatic improvements over time. They know that adaptation happens, but many do not think about adaptation unless prompted.

When I asked Sarah Lezotte to think back on her dialysis days, she focused in on those aspects of her life affected by dialysis—that same focusing illusion I discussed earlier, the one that is so hard to get rid of. She also seemed to dismiss the idea that she had adapted to life on dialysis. But she, too, could be prodded to think about her emotional resilience. When she recounted her past misery and lamented about her inability to go on if not for her hope for a transplant, I asked her to think about what she would have done if she found out she could not receive a transplant. She quickly reappraised her situation. "I imagine I would have found some way to deal with that, but I don't know how," she replied. People intuitively grasp the idea of adaptation. They just may not know how it happens.

Sarah knows more about what it is like to live with kidney failure than I will ever learn. Yet despite this knowledge, gained through such prolonged experience, she is susceptible to the same tricks of memory and imagination as the rest of us. What was it like to be on dialysis? I do not think she can answer that question very easily. Perhaps if I had filmed a day in her life while she was on dialysis and played it back to her, she could have given a more accurate report of her emotional life at that time. But I am doubtful that even that would work. What would any of us make of such a film? Would we watch ourselves brushing our teeth and cleaning dishes and assume that we must have been having a miserable day?

Sarah Lezotte is a remarkable woman. She has maintained an optimistic view of life despite everything she has been through and even plans to do more charitable work once she recovers completely from her new kidney transplant. Sixty-eight years old, with the best health she has experienced in a decade, she hopes to get out of the house and give something back to the world. I totally admire her for the way she has fought through all her health problems. And I wish her the best of luck in achieving her new goals. Meanwhile, I will try not to think about the problems that she might encounter en route to the decade of charitable activities that she envisions. I don't even want to consider the possibility that her new kidney will fail, or that at the age of sixty-eight, some new illness will enter her life and prevent her from living out her dream. Nor will I let myself think of the likelihood that she will emotionally adapt to her kidney transplant—that she will soon get used to the joys of vegetables and bananas and iced tea, taking them for granted, and, one day at a time, putting off that dream of doing charitable work. I won't let myself think about this. I don't even want to imagine the possibility.

3

Happiness: Circumstance or DNA?

Nine-year-old Jay Schreiner was too stubborn for his own good, defiantly wading across the river to retrieve his fishing pole even though his dad had warned him that the river was too dangerous to cross in the heavy rain. Jay had crossed the river hundreds of times and found it hard to believe that a little bit of rain would pose a problem. But to his surprise, he felt his feet slipping out from under him about halfway across the river. His surprise quickly turned to terror as he realized he couldn't reestablish his footing. He screamed for help while struggling to keep his head above water. Hearing his screams, Jay's dad raced in after him. But soon, like Jay, he was caught up in the powerful current. The force of the water carried Jay and his father downstream, pushing them close to shore but never close enough to regain their footing. Then Jay saw his neighbors standing in the water preparing to catch him. He reached out and grabbed hold of their arms, and they yanked him out of the river.

But no one was able to rescue Jay's father, who drowned that day trying to save the life of his stubborn son.

In the more than fifty years since his father died, Jay has not had an easy life. By all accounts, Jay was a wild child, causing trouble in school, causing even more trouble out of school, and giving everyone the impression he was throwing his life away. For a while Jay seemed to shake off his bad luck. He graduated from college, got a job as a stockbroker, and fell in love with a girl named Mary Lou. He got married and moments later (at least in retrospect) found himself chasing three children around on his bright suburban lawn.

But Jay lost his footing again, and his picture-perfect suburban life was swept away. He and Mary Lou grew apart. One by one his kids grew up and moved out west to the mountains where the family had gone each year to ski. When the last child moved west, so did Mary Lou, leaving Jay with a broken marriage and an empty nest.

Once again, Jay struggled to put his life back together. He put in time at work and hung out with his friends at a local restaurant. While hanging out at the restaurant, he met an attractive woman named Mary Beth. "But call me M.B.," she said. Several years later they got married, leaving Jay, at age fifty-nine, happier than he had been in years.

But bad luck hunted Jay down once again. Two months after his wedding, Jay felt pressure building up in his neck. He went to see his primary care doctor, who was concerned that Jay's thyroid was acting up. The thyroid blood tests were normal, but Jay's chest x-ray revealed a massive lung tumor spreading up into his neck, near his spinal cord. Based on the x-ray and the results of a biopsy, Jay's doctors told him he had incurable lung cancer. Chemotherapy wouldn't help. And surgery would merely slow the tumor down, reducing the chance that it would imminently invade his spinal cord. If Jay were lucky, the surgery could extend his life for a year or two.

So, two months into their marriage, Jay and M.B. entered the University of Pennsylvania Hospital unsure whether Jay would survive the arduous operation his doctors had planned for him, a twelve-hour procedure in which his neurosurgeon would cut out as much of Jay's tumor as possible while doing his best to spare Jay's spinal cord and the surrounding nerves. To M.B., the twelve hours that Jay spent in the operating room felt like twelve weeks, but finally she was allowed back at Jay's side, where he groggily told her he was going to be okay. M.B. and Jay breathed a sigh of relief, encouraged that Jay had made it through the operation without sustaining any obvious nerve damage. But their sense of relief was short-lived. In the hours following Jay's operation, Jay's luck changed again—only this time no one could say whether it had changed for the better or for the worse. Jay's doctors had looked at his tumor under the microscope and concluded that it wasn't lung cancer after all. It was a chordoma.

"A chorwhata?" Jay wondered. His doctors explained that when Jay was inside his mother's womb, some of his embryologic cells, which were supposed to turn into bone cells or nerve cells or something else, had instead lingered near his spinal cord in an embryonic state. Sometime in the last ten years, the cells began to grow slowly, very slowly, climbing up Jay's neck and encroaching on the nerves in his neck and the blood vessels heading up toward his brain. Eventually, this cancerous chordoma would either paralyze Jay from the neck down by pinching his spinal cord, or it would cause a fatal stroke by shutting off the blood supply to his brain. How long this would take was anyone's guess; chordomas are extremely rare. Jay traveled to a series of specialists around the country, looking for advice on how to treat his chordoma. No one even discussed *curing* Jay of his chordoma. The best they could do was to delay the day at which it would destroy one or another of Jay's vital life functions.

Is Happiness a Matter of Circumstance?

Experience has taught all of us that happiness is often a matter of circumstance. When people receive compliments from their bosses, they are happy. When they strain their lower backs shoveling snow, they are miserable. When they come inside after straining their backs and find out that their spouses are hoping to "snuggle," well . . . the cosmic irony of the situation only goes so far in improving their moods.

Recognizing that happiness is often a matter of circumstance, healthy people usually imagine that chronic illness or disability would make them miserable. They think about how miserable they feel when they experience a short-term health problem, like a case of the flu or even a stubbed toe, and conclude that long-term health problems would make them feel that way for a longer period of time.

Yet we have already seen that many people overestimate the long-term emotional impact of good and bad circumstances. They think about how elated they feel on the first warm spring day and assume they would feel equally elated if the weather was always so nice, ignoring the likelihood that they would take sunny weather for granted after a while if they lived in a place like San Diego. They are ecstatic the first time their favorite basketball team wins the NBA championship but are surprised at how much less thrilled they are when their team wins for a third straight time. Newly minted college professors labor frantically in hopes of achieving tenure, convinced that failing to do so will guarantee professional ruin and emotional doom. But research has shown that tenure decisions have no discernable effect on their long-term happiness. People who fail to receive tenure are distraught for a while but soon recover. The relationship between circumstances and emotions is often quite strong in the short run but much weaker in the long run.

Some experts contend that circumstances rarely have long-lasting effects on people's emotional lives, pointing out that even important, life-defining events like tenure decisions do not influence people's long-term happiness. But other experts do not go so far, concluding instead that very few *single* events have a major long-term impact on people's happiness because life is full of so many events and so many different circumstances. When an assistant professor is denied tenure, he imagines he will suffer years of misery. But then he is likely to find another job, perhaps at a much friendlier university. He might have a few children or get a book published that he hadn't had time to complete at his first job. Over time, and in response to all these other circumstances, he becomes as happy as he would have been if he had received tenure. Before dismissing the importance of circumstances in people's emotional lives, we should entertain the idea that specific events usually have transient effects on people's emotions because people experience so many different events in their lives.

Indeed, some college professors are miserable despite receiving tenure and others are happy despite being rejected for tenure. This disconnection between circumstances and happiness could arise because circumstances don't matter, and people's emotional lives result from their underlying personalities and not (except in extreme situations) because of their good or bad fortune.

Figuring out the role that circumstances play in people's happiness is no simple task. We all know people like Jay Schreiner, who experience more than their fair share of bad luck. Can we conclude that the unhappiness they experience is due to their unfortunate circumstances? Or are some people genetically programmed to be less happy than others, with a natural disposition to wallow in misery? How much of our happiness is due to circumstance and how much is a product of our DNA?

Some People Have All the Luck

In trying to figure out whether people's emotions are hardwired in their DNA, scientists have been able to draw upon a nice feature of DNA—its permanence. People don't change their DNA from year to year, so if DNA has any influence on people's moods, then this influence should persist over their life spans. Indeed, when researchers have assessed people's moods over many years, they have found an impressive amount of emotional stability. People who are happier than average as thirty-year-olds tend to be happier than average as forty-year-olds, fifty-year-olds, and sixty-year-olds.

Does this stability prove that happiness is, in large part at least, genetic? Consider Jay Schreiner's life. Suppose I told you that Jay was unhappy throughout the majority of his adult life. Would this make you think he had inherited unhappy DNA? Or would it simply conjure up images of all the bad luck he has encountered in his life? Unhappy as a young man because of the death of his father, unhappy later because of a rocky marriage, and unhappy now because of a chordoma? Having experienced more tragedy than most people encounter in their lives, his unhappiness could result from a string of bad circumstances.

Jay Schreiner's story illustrates that most circumstances do not occur solely by chance. Indeed, when researchers survey people over time, they not only find that happy thirty-year-olds tend to become happy forty-year-olds but also discover that happy thirty-year-olds tend to have more good things happen to them between ages thirty and forty than do unhappy thirty-year-olds.

The nonrandomness of circumstances is hardly surprising. People who are popular in high school are likely to be popular later in life. Individuals who drop out of high school typically have more difficulty finding high-paying jobs than those who graduate from college. People who lose their jobs are more likely to experience subsequent marital difficulties and health problems than those who remain employed. Good circumstances beget good circumstances, and bad circumstances beget bad ones.

How Personality Influences Circumstances

What creates this biblical-sounding cycle of begetting and begetting? Sanna Eronen, a psychologist at the University of Helsinki, believes that some people experience more good circumstances than others because of their underlying personalities.

To test this belief, Eronen asked a group of college students to look at a cartoon picturing a nondescript woman watching TV. The cartoon caption read "Carol remembers she needs to hand in an assignment to her teacher." Eronen asked students to predict what this cartoon character would do. In a follow-up cartoon, Eronen told students that the woman in the cartoon had handed in the assignment and had received her grade, and she asked students to explain what happened. In interpreting these cartoons, Eronen found that some students exhibited a generally optimistic view of the cartoon character as hardworking, smart, able to turn off a TV, and only likely to fail the assignment if it was unjustifiably difficult. Other students had a consistently low opinion of the cartoon character, saying she was a lazy, TV-watching idiot who could only pass an assignment if it was an extremely easy one. Based on these results, Eronen's study is only mildly interesting, at best, revealing that people vary in how they interpret ambiguous cartoons.

But the study is much more interesting, because five years later Eronen measured the number of good and bad events that happened in these students' lives and discovered that those students who put a positive spin on the cartoon character experienced a higher number of positive life events and a lower number of negative events than other students. In Eronen's view, when students interpreted the cartoons, they revealed something about their underlying personalities—whether they were optimists or pessimists—and about how they faced mundane challenges, like having to turn off a TV to finish a school assignment. And the personalities they revealed in this brief thought exercise revealed enough about their underlying characters to predict their fates over the next five years.

Eronen's study seems to show that personality influences the kinds of circumstances people experience. If this is true, then we have a new explanation for why people like Jay Schreiner experience a disproportionate share of rotten circumstances. They experience lots of tragedy not because bad circumstances beget other bad circumstances but because personality begets circumstance, and they happened to inherit the kind of personality that attracts misfortune.

But let's look a bit more closely at Eronen's study. In measuring the number of good and bad events that happened to these students over the five-year period, Eronen relied on the students to classify the events they experienced as being either good or bad. Given how differently these students interpreted the same little cartoon, isn't it possible that they subsequently experienced similar events, but simply interpreted them differently, with some graduating from college to take what they consider to be thrilling jobs as entry-level accountants and others taking the same jobs but perceiving them as awful luck? To answer this question, we need to explore the relationship between personality and circumstances in more depth, beginning with a series of studies by psychologist Sonia Lyubomirsky that reveal the fascinating ways that happy and unhappy people respond to identical circumstances.

How People Interpret Circumstances

Think back to when you applied to colleges. An envelope would arrive in the mail, and you would hold it in your hands, wondering whether its small size meant that the college had rejected you. Then you'd open it up (or your mother opened it if you were too nervous!). And no matter what you thought of that college, regardless of whether it was your top choice or a "safety school," the words inside the envelope would make or break your day. But what happened to your attitudes over the next few days or weeks, as the letters trickled in, a mix of good and bad news that struck at the core of your high school identity?

Lyubomirsky assessed students' attitudes before and after they applied to college and discovered that their underlying dispositions not only influenced how they responded to such news, but also influenced how they perceived the schools that accepted or rejected them.

In her study, Lyubomirsky solicited the attitudes of high school students both before and after they received their college acceptance and rejection letters. At the start of the study, she selected those students who were either much happier than average or much less happy than average. She found that happy and unhappy students had very different ways of interpreting their circumstances.

To illustrate her findings, imagine that a happy-go-lucky student learns that he did not get into Princeton, his college of choice, and decides to attend the flagship university of his home state, let's call it Home U. What will happen to his opinion of the two schools? His academic assessment of Princeton and Home U will be unchanged. But his opinion of the nonacademic side of the two schools will change. He'll come to "realize" that Home U is much more fun than Princeton.

Now imagine a second student, a chronic malcontent who experiences the same fate as our happy-go-lucky friend. Like his happy peer, he will view Home U as being more fun than he previously viewed it, but his assessment of its academic standards will decline. Like Groucho Marx, who stated that he wouldn't want to belong to any club that would have him as a member, this student will look down on Home U, while holding Princeton up as an unobtainable ideal, just as fun and academically rigorous as he had ever thought it to be.

Lyubomirsky's study showed that happy students interpreted acceptances and rejections in ways that enhanced their self-esteem. When they were rejected from a school, they protected their self-esteem by convincing themselves that the school had high academic standards and they reduced their disappointment by convincing themselves that the school would not have been much fun. By contrast, unhappy students interpreted acceptances and rejections in ways that did not enhance their self-esteem, downgrading their opinions of the academic standards of schools that accepted them, almost as if they subconsciously sought a way to continue wallowing in their misery.

What Does Self-Esteem Have to Do with It?

Happy students experienced the same circumstances as unhappy students but interpreted these circumstances differently in ways that put a positive light on their situation while promoting their self-esteem. But if their self-esteem hadn't been on the line, would happy students have interpreted circumstances any differently than unhappy students? What happens to happy and unhappy people when they experience a disappointment that has no relationship to their underlying talents, a disappointment that should have no connection to their self-esteem?

To find out, Lyubomirsky performed another clever study. She asked people to look at pictures and descriptions of a series of desserts and to rank them from most desirable to least. Then, she offered people desserts that they had individually listed as their second or third favorite. She was interested in finding out how receipt of these desserts influenced people's attitudes toward the desserts.

Imagine two people, one happy by nature and the other unhappy, who have listed their top three desserts as cheesecake, ice cream, and banana cream pie. Lyubomirsky discovered that the happy person, upon receiving the banana cream pie, will typically rate it more highly than she had previously rated it. By contrast, the unhappy person will no longer think as highly of the banana cream pie. The happy person will be happier at receiving her third choice than the unhappy person and will even reevaluate this third choice in a more favorable light, turning what could have been a mild disappointment into a pleasant surprise. The unhappy person, by contrast, will not only lower her opinion of the banana cream pie but will also lower her opinion of the desserts she did not receive, including the one she had previously rated as her favorite.

The unhappy person resorts to sour grapes thinking—like the fox who jumps and jumps to reach the grapes and who decides, when he cannot get them, that "the grapes were probably sour anyway." Such thinking might sound like a good defense mechanism, reducing unhappy people's disappointment at receiving their third favorite dessert by enabling them to believe that their top two choices weren't as spectacular as they had once seemed. But such thinking can sour people's views of the world. By the end of Lyubomirsky's experiment, for example, the unhappy people who already started out with *lower* opinions of these desserts than happy people developed even lower opinions of all the desserts. Happy people, by contrast, started off with more favorable opinions of the desserts and continued to hold these favorable opinions, despite the mild disappointment of receiving their third favorite dessert. Maybe a lifelong pattern of sour grapes thinking perpetuates unhappiness, causing all of life's joys to be diminished.

I introduced this dessert study as an example of how happy and unhappy people relate to disappointments that have nothing to do with their self-esteem. But is that the case? Lyubomirsky wondered whether happy and unhappy people differ in their interpretation of whether random events are related to their self-worth. She tested this hypothesis by conducting a follow-up dessert study. As with the previous study, she asked people to rate desserts before and after receiving their third favorite one. However, unlike the previous study, she asked people to conduct a thought experiment before making their final judgments of the desserts. She asked half of the people to reflect on their own character, "who you are and who you strive to be," and asked the other half to reflect on random topics, like "the shape of California."

What did she find? When distracted by being asked to think about the shape of California, unhappy people ended up behaving like *happy* ones. When they received their third favorite dessert, they no longer resorted to sour grapes thinking but instead continued to hold high opinions of their top three desserts, including the banana cream pie! This suggests that when unhappy people experience disappointments, they interpret these events as a reflection of themselves, unless they are distracted by a bunch of miscellaneous thought exercises.

Not convinced? Then consider what happened to the happy people. When asked to think about the shape of California, they responded to their third favorite dessert much the way they responded in the earlier study—without any need to resort to sour grapes thinking. But when mired in self-reflection, happy people ended up responding to their third favorite dessert as if they were unhappy people, resorting to sour grapes thinking. Left to their own devices, happy people do not let small, random disappointments alter their self-esteem, whereas unhappy people tend to think "It is always about me!"

I began this chapter asking whether happiness was more a matter of circumstance or a product of people's DNA. But after seeing Lyubomirsky's research, the case for circumstances has weakened. It is now clear that people's personalities influence how they interpret and respond to their circumstances.

But What Does It Mean to Have a Happy Personality?

So far, in discussing the relationship between personality and happiness, I have glossed over the notion of just what personality is. Psychologists have made great progress over the last thirty years in understanding and defining personality. Personalities are complex things, and personality psychology is a topic too large to do justice to in a few pages. Nevertheless, to understand how people respond to adversity, it is important to have an idea of how psychologists have come to understand personality.

Psychologists start out with the same basic idea of personality that you and I hold. We think of some people as being shy and others as being gregarious; some are optimists and others are pessimists. We sense that some people, even from a young age, are more stubborn than others, or more energetic, or more social, or more open-minded. Each of these traits seems relatively fixed. We are not shocked when someone changes religions in adult life, but we are surprised when a people-lover turns into a recluse.

Indeed, when first trying to measure "personality types," psychologists used natural language dictionaries to generate a list of potential personality traits. The list grew to around two hundred traits, including such attributes as gregariousness, sensation seeking, vigor, cognitive rigidity, help seeking, and emotional expressivism.

Personality psychologists developed ways to measure these traits. Using these measures, they were able to show that some people are more focused on sensation seeking than others and that such sensation seeking was stable—people who were more motivated by sensation seeking behaviors as thirty-year-olds usually remained above average on this trait as fifty-year-olds.

When trying to understand the relationship between things like personality and happiness, however, it is awfully difficult to tease apart the relative influence of two hundred personality traits. Consequently, psychologists tried to see whether they could lump the various traits into a smaller group of "über traits," so to speak. They lumped the traits together through a process known as factor analysis—essentially, they figured out which traits hung together, statistically speaking. This is a messy process, but researchers, using very different data sets and even different sets of traits, have come to very similar conclusions about the best general ways to characterize people's personalities, a lumping colloquially referred to as "the big five."

The big five personality traits that bubble up from all these statistical analyses are most commonly referred to as:

1. Extraversion—roughly characterized as the quantity and intensity of personal relationships
2. Agreeableness—the quality of personal relations, such as whether they are characterized by trust and cooperation
3. Conscientiousness—people's ability to control their impulses and organize their environments
4. Neuroticism—roughly speaking, people's emotional stability
5. Openness to experience—perhaps the most controversial of the five traits, including components such as intelligence and creativity

The big five were initially grouped together because the components of each trait hung together statistically. But the credibility of the big five has been bolstered by numerous studies showing that people's personality traits tend to remain relatively stable over long periods of time as opposed to moods, which change frequently. Their credibility has also been bolstered—their validity confirmed—by hosts of studies showing that people's personality traits predict many things about them, such as the jobs they are likely to pursue and the number and closeness of friendships they are likely to develop.

Most relevant to our purposes, the big five personality traits have been shown to predict happiness. People high in extraversion, for example, experience good moods more often than others. People with high levels of neuroticism, on the other hand, experience negative moods more often than others. Openness to experience is associated with above average frequencies of both good and bad moods, a finding that makes sense, because people high on this personality trait are willing to expose themselves to a broad range of experiences. They sample life vigorously and, therefore, experience many highs and lows.

The same circumstances have a wide range of effects on people's moods depending, in part, on their personalities. Happy people respond differently than unhappy ones. Optimists interpret circumstances differently than pessimists, and that difference leads to disparate emotional responses to otherwise similar circumstances. Some people receive a cup of water and think it is half-full whereas others think it is half-empty. We are all aware of these different types of personalities. But when it comes to thinking about illness and disability, it is easy to forget the role that personality plays in people's happiness. We imagine what it would be like to have a severe illness or disability and assume it would make us miserable, as if circumstances determine how happy we are.

However, personality plays a big role in how people respond to struggles brought on by circumstances such as illness and disability. Among people undergoing bypass surgery for coronary artery disease, for example, optimists have significantly better outcomes than pessimists. Among women newly diagnosed with breast cancer, personality goes a long way in predicting how they will cope with their illness.

Being Jay Schreiner

Imagine, for example, what it would feel like to be Jay Schreiner. Fatherless since age nine, his family of twenty-some years is now living three thousand miles away in the mountains of Montana, while he and his new wife try to figure out how to cope with a terminal illness so rare that most physicians probably do not even know how to spell it.

C-h-o-r-d-o-m-a. Fewer than fifteen hundred people in the United States have ever been diagnosed with a chordoma. Most physicians will never see a patient with this disease in their careers. It is so rare that drug companies have little incentive to invest money looking for a cure and so uncommon that it is nearly impossible to enroll enough people into clinical trials to find out what works. Rare diseases are scary. Ask people to imagine that they have either of two equally serious diseases, and they will be significantly more worried about the rare disease. People are frightened by the unknown.

It is difficult to imagine what it would feel like to be Jay Schreiner. Obviously, it must feel horrible to find out you have a chordoma. Yet, I have tried to imagine how Jay felt at that time and I cannot summon those emotions. I cannot really know how it felt. I think of the most painful emotions I have ever felt, multiply them by two or four, and convince myself that I have some idea of what it would be like to be Jay.

But am I even beginning to imagine what is going on inside Jay's head? Or am I imagining what it would be like if Peter Ubel experienced what Jay had experienced? The philosopher Thomas Nagel wrote a provocative essay many years ago pondering what it would feel like to be a bat. He concluded, after much subtle argument, that people have no way to imagine life as a bat. The best we can do is to imagine ourselves hanging upside-down, blind to our conventional senses and with an overwhelming desire to fly around at nighttime eating insects. Of course, Jay Schreiner is more like the rest of us than any bat could be. And we all have a basic enough shared understanding of human emotion to begin to conjure up an idea of what it might feel like to be Jay. But none of us is Jay. And people's personalities, as we have just learned, play a crucial role in how they interpret and respond to favorable and unfavorable circumstances.

So how has Jay responded to life with a chordoma?

He has responded the same way that Jay has responded to every setback in his life—with exuberant chatter and unrelenting optimism. I have told you a little bit about Jay's life—about his father dying, his first wife and his three children moving to Montana, and his embryologic chordoma cells re-awakening in the worst of all places. But I haven't told you a *thing* about Jay.

Jay Schreiner is one of the happiest people I have ever met. He simply exudes positive energy. Jay is also a social animal, with a huge network of devoted friends. In psychologic parlance, he is high in extraversion. Put him in a room full of strangers, and he'll make a few friends before the night is over, not because he is schmoozing people for secondary gain but because he is genuinely interested in everything about everyone: "You bought a used car?" he might say. "Well, where did you get it? Have you had any problems with it? . . . Hearing a strange sound, hmmm. . . . Maybe it is the distributor cap. Let's go take a look."

I got a taste of Jay's personality one day when he gave me a tour of his neighborhood, a cluster of old stone homes about forty-five minutes outside of Philadelphia. We first walked across the street to look at a house that was in the middle of renovation. The homeowner welcomed us inside enthusiastically, clearly happy to have Jay visiting. Jay joked with her while we wandered from room to room. In a second story bedroom we ran into two of the renovators who were fixing some windows. Jay immediately engaged them in conversation about the kind of materials they were using and about some interesting work he had seen them do in other rooms. By the time we left the house, he had two new friends.

From that house, Jay whisked me around the corner where he simply had to show me another house being renovated. The homeowner and his father were inside doing some electrical work when we arrived. They gladly put down their work and showed me the house while Jay chatted with them. To describe me as having no talent at or interest in home repair jobs is an understatement, but on that day I was swept up by Jay's enthusiasm and by the friendliness of his neighbors. For ten or fifteen minutes I could almost tell the difference between a two-by-four and a four-by-four. By the time we made it back to Jay's house, I think I had met the whole neighborhood and everyone, young and old, seemed to be best friends with Jay.

When we arrived at Jay's house, his wife had just returned home from running some errands. You wouldn't put Jay and M.B. together based on superficial characteristics. About twenty years younger than Jay, M.B. is tall, slim, and attractive with a business degree and a sharp sense of humor. Jay, on the other hand, is not exactly a male model. He is medium height, on his tiptoes, with a stocky frame hiding underneath a layer of padding. M.B. was not attracted to Jay because of his looks, although she does think he is adorable. Instead, she was simply overwhelmed by Jay's personality. M.B. was manager at a restaurant that Jay frequented with friends after his wife moved to Montana. M.B. noticed Jay because he always seemed to be smiling and because whoever came in with him usually ended up spending most of the evening laughing. She became good friends with Jay, feeling so comfortable talking with him that she'd read him the love letters she would get from her long-distance boyfriend to get his insights.

Like his chordoma, which resided inside him from the time he was an embryo, Jay's exuberance has the feel of an inborn trait. His long-term mood seems almost impervious to circumstance. His emotional recovery from adversity comes off like some kind of spinal cord reflex—automatic and hardwired.

Nevertheless, Jay's hyperkinetic optimism has been put to a very severe test by the slow and steady progress of his chordoma. The neurosurgeon who operated on Jay shortly after his tumor was discovered spent twelve hours trying to remove the tumor. But its delicate strands weaved tortuously around Jay's neck and upper chest and were often indiscernible from the normal tissue it was invading, making it impossible to remove the entire tumor without removing

a vital nerve or blood vessel. So, after Jay recovered from the operation, he underwent an aggressive course of radiation treatment in
hopes of slowing down the tumor even more.

When these arduous treatments were finished, Jay had no idea
what to expect from his chordoma—how fast it would grow and
which important bodily functions it would threaten. So he tried to
live life as normally as possible, keeping his job as a stockbroker and
reminding himself that he was still a newlywed, with a wife he had
better start spending quality time with as soon as possible.

Unfortunately, the tumor quickly made its presence known again.
In a matter of months, Jay began experiencing sharp pains as the
chordoma wrapped itself around the sensory nerves exiting his
spinal cord. Some of his pains were constant—a hot sensation in
his right hand that burned from the inside out as if someone stuck
his hand in a microwave and a pain in his right shoulder that struck
every time he turned to the left. Other pains were maddeningly
unpredictable, sending electric jolts down either arm when pro-
voked by random movements. The tumor also infiltrated Jay's sym-
pathetic nerves, causing his left eye to droop and his left pupil to
dilate, giving half his face the oxymoronic look of someone who is
simultaneously startled and half-asleep. The tumor infiltrated Jay's
motor nerves too, slowly chewing away at the muscles enervating
his right hand. He began to lose strength in his right arm, and he
became scared, really scared. He could ignore the pain, or at least
minimize it through the strength of his will. But he could not
ignore the weakness or risk experiencing the kind of damage that
doesn't respect willpower.

So Jay called his neurosurgeon and described his symptoms, a
phone conversation that made him feel once again like a stubborn
little boy. The surgeon gave him a severe tongue lashing for waiting
so long to call. Jay went back under the knife the next day with his
surgeon cutting out the tumorous strands responsible for Jay's newest
symptoms. This second operation reduced Jay's pain but did not

restore his strength. In response, Jay began to carry a squeezy ball in his pocket to strengthen the remaining muscles in his right hand.

Fortunately, Jay has never delayed communicating with his doctors since being reprimanded that day. Unfortunately, he has had plenty of occasions to talk with them about the many symptoms caused by his relentless tumor. In fact, Jay has now battled his chordoma for more than ten years, with eleven neurosurgical procedures to date. His battle has settled into a kind of rhythm. Jay goes in for surgery, comes home and recovers, feels better for a while, and then begins experiencing new symptoms, which he quickly reports to his surgeon. With narcotics to help with the pain, Jay and his surgeon monitor the symptoms for a while until they reach a point where it is time for another operation. Jay then returns to the University of Pennsylvania for his next surgical procedure, where the anesthesiologist, who did such a good job on Jay's third operation, meets Jay and reassures him that he will use the same anesthesia he used the last time.

How Does He Do It?

How does Jay cope with the pain, disfigurement, and paralysis of his chordoma? How does he handle the likelihood that the tumor will shorten his life and prevent him from spending the decades of time he planned to spend with M.B.?

Spending time with Jay, I can construct a number of theories to explain his happiness. In part, I believe the fatality of his situation has helped Jay thrive. At the beginning of this ordeal, Jay and M.B. were convinced that the chordoma would kill Jay within a couple years, maybe even within a couple of months. They would not have acknowledged the hopelessness of Jay's situation at the time. If quizzed ten years ago, they would have emphasized the hope they held that Jay would live for many years. But no way, no how, did they believe that Jay would live for another decade or more.

Convinced that Jay would soon die, they have savored their time together. To spend more time together, they both cut back on work, never tiring of each other's company. Because of their sense of urgency, they have truly relished their time together, time that has always felt a bit borrowed, knowing, as they do, that Jay's tumor could creep up into a vital part of his anatomy at any time.

Alternatively, I would attribute Jay's resilience to the omnipresence of his illness. The weakness and pain, while causing him to suffer, also serve as a constant reminder of his illness, a reminder that he shouldn't take anything for granted. Always a head turn away from electric pain, Jay has had no chance to become complacent.

I could tell you that Jay is happy because he had put away enough money to retire early to spend time with M.B. I could ascribe his resilience to his strong religious faith, too, or to his supportive children. I could fall back on academic metaphors, crediting his psychologic immune system or marveling at his hedonic treadmill.

But I'd be lying. I can't be sure whether any of these factors contributed to Jay's resilience. I can't say whether Jay owes his happiness to M.B., his belief in Jesus, or his bank account. I *can* tell you that most people do benefit from these kinds of social, spiritual, and financial resources. Indeed, in later chapters I'll explore a host of factors that help people struggle against adversity. But what is true for a population may not be true for an individual. Religion might make many people more resilient—but not everybody.

In fact, in Jay's case I have a hard time believing any of these factors play a crucial role in his resilient response to the chordoma. As wonderful as M.B. has been for Jay, I expect other friends and relatives would have stepped into the void if she had been absent. I also suspect that Jay would have found a way to get by even without money or his church congregation. I am not suggesting that Jay is impervious to circumstances. But I am doubtful that many circumstances could overwhelm Jay's inherent optimism. To me, Jay feels constitutionally incapable of wallowing in misery.

Nature, Nurture, and Personality

As Jay Schreiner's story illustrates, the relationship between circumstances and happiness can depend on people's attitudes and personalities. In Jay's shoes, some people would retreat into their shell, "woe-is-me-ing" the last few months or years of their lives. But Jay does not a have a shell and sees no point in complaining about his lot in life. Instead, despite pain and disability, he still manages to enjoy each day more than most healthy people do.

But Jay's story does not show why some people are happy by nature and others are unhappy. It does not explain why there are optimists and pessimists, extraverts and introverts. Could it be that circumstances early in life create people's personality traits, which then influence how they interpret subsequent events? Or is personality coded in people's DNA?

In the movie *Trading Places*, a couple of old men who reek of even older money sit in the lounge of their private club debating whether people's positions in life are determined by heredity or environment. To resolve this debate, they arrange for Eddie Murphy, a street beggar, to change places with Dan Ackroyd, a wealthy investment banker who has inherited his position in life. The movie shows that Eddie Murphy's character can master any trade in a couple of weeks. But the movie has not yet been accepted by scientists as definitive evidence to resolve debates about nature versus nurture. Instead, the nature/nurture debates continue.

These debates can be exhausting and frustrating, in large part because of the implausible views held by people on either extreme. One extreme characterizes humans as slaves to the laws of physics, lacking free will of any kind. According to this view, creativity is a mirage and ethics is a waste of time, but that doesn't matter because people are all predetermined to think that creativity and morality exist! At the other extreme, humans are said to be the product of their environments; boys enjoy roughhousing more than girls not because testosterone influences their brain development and not because evolution would try to make boys and girls care about different things, but because boys and girls are treated differently by their parents, grandparents, and anyone else who interacts with them during their formative years. Such thinking can devastate parents who, despite their best efforts to raise enlightened, gender-neutral children, find that their boys like doing boy things and their girls like doing girl things.

It would be trite for me to simply contend that the truth lies somewhere between these two extremes. Instead, the real challenge is to determine *where* in the middle the truth resides. How much of our personality is determined at birth, how much by age two, and how much room is left for personalities to change after that? The relationship between personality and happiness makes this question that much more important. Is it clear, by age two, who's going to be happy? Are miserable sixth graders doomed to become miserable adults? Is there any point in striving for happiness if you have not achieved it by the time you have a driver's license?

Considering Identical Twins

One way to answer these questions is to study the happiness of identical twins. Identical twins are formed when a fertilized eggs splits into two, producing two people with nearly identical DNA (except for rare mutations that occur after the egg has split in two). If happiness levels and personality types are genetic, identical twins should have similar temperaments and personalities.

And they do! Identical twins raised together exhibit very similar levels of happiness—if one twin is happy most of the time, chances are the other one is, too. Do these similarities prove that happiness is genetic? No, they don't. Identical twins might have similar temperaments because they have similar upbringings, experiencing similar environments in their formative years—the same schools, the same neighborhoods, and the same overbearing (or underbearing?) parents.

What if we discover that the happiness of identical twins raised together is more similar than the happiness of a random sample of siblings raised together. Would *this* tell us that genetics influences personality? No, it wouldn't. The similarity of identical twins might arise because twins are raised differently than other siblings. Twins reside in the same part of the birth order, a potentially important influence on their upbringing. The first child enjoys a year or more of relatively undivided attention that later children rarely receive. Later children get to interact with older siblings in their formative years, an experience not available to first children. Thus, being raised in the same part of the birth order may cause identical twins to share similar personalities.

Being a twin also creates unique situations that most other siblings would not otherwise encounter, which might cause twins to behave alike. Early on, mothers have to breast-feed two children at a time. This clearly will leave mothers more exhausted than if they had only given birth to one new child. Twins get to share a sibling of the same exact age, too. Comparing identical twins to nontwin siblings doesn't help us figure out the role DNA plays in people's treatment.

Suppose, instead, we compare identical twins raised together to nonidentical twins raised together and find that the happiness of identical twins is more similar than that of nonidentical twins. Have we finally isolated the influence of genetics on happiness? Not yet. Parents might raise identical twins differently than nonidentical twins. Maybe parents of identical twins are more likely to treat the twins *identically*, dressing them in the same outfits, for example. Maybe parents of identical twins assume the twins will have identical personalities, and these assumptions influence the way they raise their children.

If we hope to measure the relative influence of genetics on personality, we need to compare identical and nonidentical twins raised together to those raised apart.

What do these twin studies reveal? They show that if you have an unhappy identical twin, you are probably unhappy, regardless of whether you were raised in the same household as your twin. The same holds for personality. If your identical twin is an extravert, chances are good that you're one, too, even if you were separated at birth leaving your twin with stifling parents while you were raised on a commune.

Experts estimate that 50 percent of the variation in happiness levels across people can be explained by genetics and only 20 percent by home environment (whether they were raised by one set of parents or another). The same percentages hold true for personality traits, too. In other words, if your children are happy extraverts, don't credit your parenting skills. Congratulate their DNA!

Words of Caution

Is this genetic determinism talk getting you depressed? It shouldn't. To begin with, we all know people who have dramatically turned their lives around, from misery to happiness. These people serve as reminders that the 50 percent figure is an average, meaning that some people's happiness and personalities are less than 50 percent attributable to genetics. People are not predetermined to be happy or unhappy, nor are they predetermined to be lazy or productive. Instead, they are genetically predisposed to behave and feel in certain ways, predispositions that they can overcome. Some people are dramatically happier than their identical twins.

Nor should you get depressed that all your hard parenting work was for naught, shaping only 20 percent of your children's futures. The 20 percent figure represents the difference that home environments contribute, on average, to happiness, and this 20 percent contribution exists within a society where extreme differences in parenting styles are rare. It is true that some parents are stronger disciplinarians than others, and that some parents spend more time with their children than others. But these differences are rarely extreme enough to change a happy child into a miserable one or an extravert into an introvert. In most homes, parenting does not dramatically shape children's basic personality types. But in every home, parenting influences children in thousands of other ways, shaping children's interests, beliefs, and religious affiliations—the children of Roman Catholic parents, after all, don't grow up into Roman Catholic adults because they inherit a gene for Roman Catholicism. And in rare homes, parenting has a huge effect on children's personalities and temperaments. To take an extreme example: if parents locked their children in closets eighteen hours a day, the children would grow up into miserable adults, regardless of their genetic predispositions. Environment ultimately trumps genetics. A child with happy DNA can be starved and frightened into submission.

There's another reason to be cautious about the precise estimates yielded by the twin studies: they ignore what I call "the Bilski effect." Back in high school, I played soccer with Jim and Dave Bilski, identical twins who were tall, good-looking, and smart. (One had a tiny mole on his cheek that enabled the rest of us to tell him apart from his brother. Stand on the wrong side of a Bilski and you wouldn't know if you were talking to Jim or to Dave, a fact that often created the strange spectacle of a group of kids doing their best to subtly stand on the left side of a Bilski twin until they knew which one they were talking to.) Both Bilskis were excellent soccer players. Both were very popular with girls. And both were pretty happy, as I probably would have been if I had been that good at soccer and that popular with girls. If the Bilskis had been reared apart, both would still have been tall, dark, and handsome, with intelligence and athletic ability to boot. And both would probably have been happy too, given that combination of attributes.

To understand the Bilski effect, you need to imagine that one of the tall, "good-looking" Bilskis was raised in a culture where tall and dark was not considered handsome, where he was ostracized as a freak. I'm not so sure that Bilski would exhibit such similar levels of happiness anymore. The 50 percent figure from the twins studies ignores the similarity in environments that most twins share, even when they are raised in different households. Being genetically intelligent or good-looking or athletic alters the way other people treat you.

Ultimately, the exact contribution of DNA to people's happiness or personalities might be significantly lower than 50 percent. But the general truth remains—life really is unfair and one of the greatest sources of unfairness is DNA. Some people are genetically inclined toward happiness, intelligence, optimism, and sociability, and others are not.

As Jay Schreiner's life reveals, personality can go a long way in helping people overcome extreme circumstances. Pain and paralysis need not lead to misery. But Jay's story also reminds us that no single circumstance exists in isolation. People with chordomas have lives. Earlier, I refused to credit Jay's happiness to his wealth, his religious faith, or his devoted new wife. Nevertheless, without any of these resources, it is easy to imagine Jay succumbing to circumstance.

People are not immune to circumstance, and they are not prisoners of their DNA. And when confronted with adversity, they can't hire someone to replace their DNA. To overcome difficult circumstances and to summon their emotional resilience, people often need to marshal their financial, spiritual, intellectual, and social resources. Now that we've looked at the important role genetics plays in people's emotional lives, let's turn to the nongenetic resources we can all draw upon to maximize our ability to overcome the struggles that come our way.

4

Responding to Adversity

In the weeks following his coma, Greg Hughes, whom we met in Chapter 1, did not allow himself to get depressed over the loss of his legs. If anything, his mood was downright upbeat. Friends and relatives would visit him in the rehabilitation hospital, standing dejectedly by his bedside bemoaning his fate, while Greg tried his best to cheer *them* up. Visitors were amazed at Greg's attitude, but he shrugged off their praise. He couldn't see the point of getting upset about losing his legs. "It's not like I'd get my legs back," he told me.

Greg's common sense seemed uncommonly wise. Faced with a horrific disability, he shrugged his shoulders and got on with his life.

But what accounts for Greg's resilience? Based on Chapter 3, I could say Greg was happy because he inherited happy DNA that caused his psychologic immune system to kick into action, to rid him of the negative emotions brought upon him by his disability. But even though Greg's DNA was clearly on his side, attributing his emotional resilience to DNA does not explain much about *how* Greg was able to find happiness so quickly. Nor does attributing his recovery to his psychologic immune system. If this immune system were a physical, tangible entity rather than a metaphor, scientists could uncover the secrets of how it functions, much like they have discovered how the actual immune system works. With the immune system, scientists discovered that white blood cells produce antibodies in response to foreign antigens. They have honed in on the chemical structure of these antibodies and shown how the antibodies glom onto antigens. They have even drilled down to the level of DNA to discover which genes code for the various proteins crucial to a normally functioning immune system.

No such understanding of the psychologic immune system exists at present, in large part, of course, because there *are* no emotional antibodies chasing around circumstantially induced emotional antigens. The existence of metaphors like the psychologic immune system, in fact, is good evidence that at a molecular or cellular level we don't understand how people manage to emotionally overcome difficult circumstances. We don't know which brain neurons trigger the kind of thoughts that allow people to find happiness. We don't understand the chemical cascades throughout the body that allow some people to recover faster from trauma than others.

Similarly, knowing that heredity plays a big role in people's general moods does not help us understand *why* people are happy. To say "Greg Hughes is happy because he inherited happy DNA" is not a satisfying explanation for his remarkable outlook on life. DNA doesn't make people happy directly. It does so indirectly, through the proteins that it codes, proteins that influence how people's brains are wired, wiring that then influences people's personalities and temperaments. Yet, we don't currently know what strands of DNA produce the array of proteins that lead to the cellular activities that enable people to find happiness.

But that's okay. We don't need to understand the cellular and molecular workings of the brain to understand behavior. Sometimes, in fact, higher level explanations provide more insight about people's emotions than do cellular and molecular explanations. For example, imagine you are meandering barefoot in the woods and you step on a sharp splinter. You scream in pain, bend over and pull the splinter out, rub your foot to ease the pain, and return to your car to grab a first-aid kit and a pair of shoes. There are many levels at which a scientist could try to explain your behavior. She could focus on the neurophysiology of pain, describing the chemical processes triggered by the splinter—the way your pain neurons respond to trauma, the location in the cortex of your brain that receives these pain signals, and the connections between this part of your cortex and the part of your cortex that tries to determine the source of the pain. She could drill down to a deeper level and try to figure out how your DNA was able to create pain neurons in the first place and the mechanisms by which your DNA connected your pain fibers to the correct part of your cerebral cortex.

But in either case—at the level of neurons or at the level of DNA—has she done anything to show why you walked back to the car, pulled out a tube of antibacterial cream and a Band-Aid, applied them to your foot, and covered your feet with tennis shoes? Wouldn't it be easier to explain your behavior by saying that you wanted to keep your wound clean and prevent further injury? Ultimately, scientists hope to understand human behavior at high levels and low levels. But it is not obvious that sorting the molecular details of complex behaviors will help us understand Band-Aid decision making better than we already do.

For the same reason, I don't expect to learn anytime soon which segments of Greg's DNA guided his body to make the proteins that enabled him to show such resilience, nor would I expect that knowledge to help me understand Greg's attitudes. But I could attempt to understand him, or at least begin to do so, at a different level. I could learn about Greg by visiting him in the hospital.

I first learned about the challenge of rehabilitation in my third year of medical school when I worked in a rehabilitation hospital for two months. I remember arriving at the hospital expecting to see a cozy place where people licked their wounds and exercised while physical therapists soothed them with kind words and gentle massages. I envisioned a place where people could amble back onto their feet, so to speak, and recover from their various disabilities, something like a resort spa, perhaps. I soon found out that a rehabilitation hospital more closely resembles a military boot camp.

Greg logged an average of six hours of therapy a day. None of these hours was gentle, touchy-feely therapy sessions. Greg had lots of work to do in order to learn how to function without legs. First and foremost, he had to strengthen his arms, which had atrophied during the two-and-a-half weeks he spent in a coma, so much so that when he first woke up, he was too weak to comb his hair. If he intended to become independent, he would need enough arm strength to lift himself out of bed and swing his torso into his wheelchair. He would need to master other difficult maneuvers too: chair to bed, chair to toilet, toilet to chair, chair to truck, and so on.

The physical therapists spent many hours helping Greg practice these exhausting maneuvers. They briefly applauded each of his accomplishments and then, almost without pause, introduced him to the next challenge. In addition to his physical therapy sessions, Greg spent time each day in hydrotherapy, cleaning and caring for the wounds where the surgeons had sealed off the stumps of his legs. He also spent time in occupational therapy, learning such important skills as how to get dressed. When not in physical therapy, hydro-therapy, or occupational therapy, Greg was eating, sleeping, or vis-iting with friends and family. In short, to learn how to physically deal with his new disability, Greg needed to mobilize all of his emotional strength to get through each exhausting day.

Marshaling Resources to Face Adversity

When people experience adversity, they mobilize their physiologic, emotional, and cognitive resources to confront the adversity. Let's return to the earlier example of stepping on a splinter while walk-ing barefoot in the woods. The pain of the splinter will cause stress hormones, like adrenaline and cortisol, to surge into your bloodstream, increasing your heart rate and blood pressure in the process. At the same time, these stress hormones will temporarily stop your body from digesting food and processing waste fluids; they will even put your immune system on a mini-vacation. Shutting down these vital physiologic functions allows you to mobilize your bodily resources to address the threat. Alerted to the pain, you will mobilize your cognitive resources to deal with the pain, with all your conversations and daydreams coming to a halt as you look to see why your foot hurts. By the time you pull the splinter out of your foot and clean the wound, your stress hormone levels will probably have returned to normal, unless you don't have a pair of shoes handy, at which point you'll probably remain at a state of high arousal until you reach a splinter-free zone.

When people experience negative events, they mobilize their resources to deal with the situation—focusing their attention on how to improve the situation and thinking of ways to avoid similar situations in the future. Negative emotions demand action. When people feel hungry, they look for food; when they feel angry, they tear off the head of the person they are angry at (metaphorically speaking, of course) or they figure out what else they can do to rid themselves of their angry feelings. By contrast, positive emotions rarely trigger such focused attention and energy. When people feel happiness, they don't wander around wondering why they are so happy or spend any time thinking of ways to become less happy. They simply enjoy their good fortune.

It bears repeating: negative emotions demand attention. When shown a picture of a crowd, people rapidly focus their attention on the angry faces in the crowd, not on the happy ones. People are hardwired to be attentive to and respond to threats. When making judgments about others, for example, people pay disproportionate attention to negative information. And when thinking about risky situations, most people place more weight on avoiding losses than on achieving similarly sized gains. Paying close attention to negative events is one of the ways people mobilize their cognitive resources to rid themselves of their painful emotions.

Once their attention is focused on negative events, people demonstrate the kind of critical thinking powers that often help them deal effectively with the negative events. When in bad moods, for example, people seek out information more thoroughly than when in good moods, and they evaluate arguments more critically. (When bad moods are too extreme, of course, this all breaks down. Severe anxiety and depression are not conducive to clear, focused thinking, nor do they help people deal with negative events.) When in bad moods, people often try to figure out what is causing their moods and find ways to avoid feeling that way again. Much the way a painful splinter encourages us to watch more carefully for splinters, a painful emotion motivates us to avoid circumstances that lead to emotional pain. Many successful athletes say they hate losing more than they love winning. Negative emotions are very good motivators!

When Bad Things Happen

The mobilization of physiologic and cognitive resources in response to negative events makes great evolutionary sense. When people step on splinters or hear lions stalking them, it does not make much evolutionary sense for them to empty their bladders or compose operas. People need to respond to these threats with focused attention and often with all their physiological resources. Fight or flight; do something immediate and definitive; don't daydream or waste any time.

In Greg's case, the benefits of mobilizing resources to deal with negative events are obvious. When he was in the intensive care unit, his body was struggling to overcome life-threatening infections. Later his body needed the strength to repair the wounds created in each of his seven operations. To maintain his blood pressure and give him the strength to fight, he needed every stress hormone his body could muster. And when he woke up from his coma, a burst or two of fresh hormones probably helped him muster the emotional strength to begin the arduous job of rehabilitating his badly weakened body.

But Greg's physical rehabilitation was not going to be completed in a day or two. He had months of hard work ahead. And once rehabilitated, Greg faced a lifetime of physical challenges arising from having no legs and emotional challenges arising from the stigmatization and discrimination that would inevitably accompany him wherever he went. Should Greg's body remain in high alert, fight or flight mode for the next few months? How about for the rest of his lifetime? What happens to people's bodies when they release stress hormones for long periods of time?

The High Cost of Long-Term Mobilization

Remaining in a perpetual state of high alert is bad for people's health. Stress hormones suppress people's immune systems, a good way to divert physiologic resources to urgent short-term needs but a risky thing to do for a long period of time. Stress hormones raise people's blood pressure and heart rate, also wonderful things to do in the short run when people are running away from lions, but disastrous in the long run if people hope to avoid heart attacks and strokes. In fact, people under chronic stress are prone to a whole range of illnesses, such as heart disease, depression, rheumatoid arthritis, diabetes, and stomach ulcers.

Health professionals have come full circle in their understanding of the relationship between stress and health, between "mind and body." Take stomach ulcers, for example. Before the scientific basis of most illnesses had been uncovered, most physicians were quite comfortable attributing stomach ulcers (and their close cousins, duodenal ulcers) to stress. But then in the 1970s and 1980s, medical researchers began to learn more about the physiology of the digestive tract. They learned that people's stomachs produce large amounts of acid to help them digest their food. And they developed medications that could prevent or heal stomach ulcers by reducing acid production in the stomach.

The success of these powerful new ulcer medicines, multibillion dollar products like Tagamet and Prilosec, convinced most physicians that stomach ulcers were caused by acid secretion, not by stress. After all, no one was curing stomach ulcers by lowering people's stress levels.

Eventually, however, chinks began appearing in the armor of these wonderful new ulcer medicines. The medicines did a great job of curing patients' ulcers, but once patients stopped taking the pills, the majority of them got ulcers again. Experts wondered whether these patients simply returned to their high-acid producing ways once they went off the medicines. But when they measured the patients' acid levels, they found out that most of them were not producing unusually high amounts of stomach acid. Instead, it appeared that these people's stomachs were unusually susceptible to stomach acid. But why?

Around this time, word started circulating at gastroenterology conferences of a physician who was convinced that many stomach ulcers were caused by, of all things, a newly discovered bacteria. *Helicobacter pylori* he called it, and he claimed it had been hiding out in ulcerated stomachs without physicians' knowledge. His initial claims were met with incredulity by most physicians, who were convinced that ulcers were caused by stomach acid. Once people have a theory that seems to explain their world effectively, they are usually resistant to new theories. Other physicians took this new bacteria more seriously but, quite reasonably, speculated that perhaps this bacteria, rather than causing stomach ulcers, simply grew in patients' stomachs once they had ulcers. In other words, maybe this bacteria enjoyed living in ulcers.

So, the doctor proved his theory (I'm not making this up!) by drinking a jug full of the bacteria and coming down with a whopper of a stomach ulcer. Eventually the medical establishment yielded. Ulcers weren't caused by acid anymore. They were caused by a bacteria that made people susceptible to their normal stomach acids. This shift in explanations pushed the stress theory of stomach ulcers even further into the background. Ulcers should be treated by acid suppressing medications and antibiotics, not by addressing chronic emotional stress, doctors reasoned.

But the story didn't end there. Doctors began to wonder why some people were more susceptible to *H. pylori* infections than others. The stress theory of ulcer formation was ready for a comeback: chronic stress, as we have just learned, leads to chronically elevated stress hormones, which suppress people's immune systems, which make them susceptible to bacterial infections! The circle was now complete. Physicians accepted, once again, that stress can lead to stomach ulcers!

Physicians are beginning to rethink a number of other illnesses, too. In fact, attitudes toward heart attacks and stress have also come full circle during my lifetime. When I was in high school in the late 1970s, most physicians believed that stress caused heart attacks, blaming heart disease on Type A behavior, a phrase made popular by a bestselling book. By the time I went to medical school in the mid-1980s, however, Type A behavior was nowhere to be found. Well, actually, Type A behavior was all around me, surrounded as I was by hyperdriven classmates. But Type A behavior was nowhere to be found in the *medical curriculum*. Instead, professors lectured us about the evils of cholesterol, explaining that fat cat executives were dying not because they were stressed-out by executive duties but because they were fat! Within a decade of my medical school graduation, the link between cholesterol and heart disease had been proven beyond a doubt, with huge clinical trials demonstrating that cholesterol pills could reduce the risk of heart attacks. Stress, it seemed, was going to be a symptom of the past.

Chronic Stress

But stress was not prepared to become an historical oddity. Researchers began to notice strange things. People under chronic stress, at home or at work, still develop high rates of heart disease, higher in fact than can be explained by their blood pressure, cholesterol levels, smoking habits, or exercise routines. Experts increasingly recognized that chronically elevated stress hormones wreak havoc on people's hearts. In rare cases, hormone levels become so high that they cause acute heart failure, a phenomenon dubbed the broken heart syndrome. More frequently, chronic stress increases people's chances of developing coronary artery disease—blockages of the small arteries that supply blood to the heart. Simply put, chronic stress is bad for people's health.

As bad as chronic stress can be for people's health, it is not always possible to avoid chronically stressful circumstances. When Greg Hughes first became sick, his stress hormones were invaluable in helping him rehabilitate his battered body. But his legs are now gone forever, and if he responds now by feeling chronically stressed out, the burdens of his stress hormones will soon outweigh the benefits. What can Greg do to reel in his stress hormones? What can he do to minimize his emotional pain?

Fortunately, Greg is not the first person to experience a chronic stressor. Some of our evolutionary predecessors undoubtedly experienced chronically stressful circumstances, such as droughts or long winters or conflict with rivals for mates. A Homo erectus who could find ways of dealing with chronically negative events without relying on a constant release of stress hormones would have an evolutionary advantage over one who could not.

Silver Lining Thinking

When people experience pain, they mobilize their cognitive resources to determine the source of their pain ("a splinter . . . that must be what hurts so much"), to find ways to remove the cause of the pain ("I better take this splinter out"), and to think about ways to avoid reexperiencing the pain ("Hmmm, maybe I should wear shoes next time!"). But they also take additional measures to minimize their pain immediately. If people accomplish everything they can accomplish by mobilizing their resources, they might as well find a way to feel good again.

Researchers have learned that when people experience painful emotions, they find creative ways to minimize their pain. They distract themselves from their misfortunes, perhaps by visiting with friends or pursuing pleasurable activities. When distraction fails, they find ways to convince themselves that their misfortunes are not really so serious. For example, a man criticized by his boss might minimize the impact of that criticism by attributing it to forces beyond his control—deciding that his work performance was subpar because of a colleague's interference, for instance. People also find ways of putting bad circumstances out of their minds. Studies of memory show that people have a disproportionately hard time remembering negative—as opposed to positive—experiences, and that they often reinterpret negative experiences so that they are remembered as being less awful than they really were.

People also minimize their emotional pain by looking for silver linings in what appear to be the darkest of clouds. In the 1980s, Susan Folkman, a health psychologist at the University of California San Francisco, learned just how important such silver linings can be. Folkman is one of the world's experts on how people cope with difficult circumstances. She got together with some colleagues to interview people who were taking care of loved ones dying of AIDS. Folkman was trying to understand the difficulties caregivers encounter under such trying circumstances. But as the study progressed, she was deluged with complaints from the caregivers who wondered why the researchers weren't asking them about any of the *good* things resulting from their situations. Many caregivers were adamant that, even though it was emotionally and physically exhausting to take care of a dying loved one, caregiving was primarily a positive experience, bringing them closer to their loved ones and bringing meaning and purpose to their lives.

This type of silver lining thinking is just as pervasively exhibited by people themselves experiencing chronic illnesses or disabilities. Some patients with spinal cord injuries say that their injuries have strengthened their character. Many people with cancer or diabetes or heart failure say that their illnesses have clarified their life goals and have made them take life more seriously. But this silver lining thinking isn't simply a result of creative reinterpretations of otherwise dismal situations. Many people, in fact, *have* had their lives improved by illness or disability. Seven-time Tour de France winner Lance Armstrong fulfilled his bicycling potential only after nearly succumbing to metastatic testicular cancer. A promising, but undisciplined, rider at the time of his diagnosis, he came back from his treatment with a much better idea of what he wanted to accomplish in his life.

Of course, Armstrong is a bit unusual—he enjoys bicycle racing *because* of all the pain associated with it. Still, his view that an awful illness actually improved his life is not unique to masochistic bicyclists. Take, for example, the words—as reported in a medical article by G. L. Albrecht—of a young man disabled in a knife fight:

When I was eighteen, I thought it was cool to be a gang-banger. Everyone gave you respect, girls were always around, and money was easy. Then, I got knifed in a fight. I didn't know it right away but I was partly paralyzed. Lying in the bed at Cook County, I thought about what's so great about belonging to a gang. I have a mom and two younger sisters at home. They need help and a different example. I went back to get a GED, and I'm trying to help my mom and keep my sisters in school and off the street.

As Greg Hughes busied himself with his daily therapies, he did not minimize his emotional pain by resorting to silver lining thinking because at least at the time he could not think of any way his life had been improved by losing his legs. And yet, within a couple of weeks of waking up from his coma, Greg had already found ways to minimize his emotional pain, often describing his amputations with phrases like "this little setback." In part, he minimized his emotional pain by visiting with friends and family, by immersing himself in his therapy sessions, and by refusing to dwell on the past. And his efforts at minimizing his pain did not stop there. Visiting Greg in the hospital, I was struck by how often he adopted what psychologists call "counterfactual thinking." He pondered what might have happened rather than what actually happened, and this made him feel better.

The Dark Side of Counterfactual Thinking

Counterfactual thinking is not always a good way for people to find happiness after they experience bad circumstances. To use a mundane example: imagine two people traveling to the airport. Both are caught in unpredictably bad traffic and arrive at the airport thirty minutes after their scheduled departure time. The first person's plane leaves on time, meaning that he is thirty minutes late for his flight. Although unhappy about missing his flight, he probably will not be bothered very much by counterfactual thinking. The second person's plane, on the other hand, leaves twenty-five minutes late, meaning that he misses his flight by only five minutes. The second person will be plagued by counterfactual thoughts, pondering the traffic light he barely missed near the end of his drive or the five minutes of Katie Couric he watched before leaving for the airport. "Why didn't I run that yellow light? Why didn't I leave after hearing about the weather in my neck of the woods?"

As a lifelong Minnesota Vikings fan, I have suffered the ill effects of counterfactual thinking on many occasions, most notably in 1998, when they were heavily favored to beat the Atlanta Falcons in the NFC title game. The game turned out to be closer than expected. In the last seconds of the fourth quarter, with the game tied, the Vikings moved into field goal range and their placekicker, Gary Anderson, lined up to kick what would be a game-winning field goal. Anderson had not missed a field goal all season long, and this particular field goal attempt was well within his range. But Anderson's kick drifted wide of the crossbars, and the game went into overtime.

Atlanta got hold of the ball in overtime and drove into field goal range. Football overtimes are sudden death events, so if Atlanta kicked a field goal, they would win the game and go to the Super Bowl and my beloved Vikings would lose again. The Atlanta field goal attempt was nothing more than a chip shot. I could not even bear to watch as their placekicker lined up to kick the ball. My wife, Paula, walked into the room around this time and saw me with my head buried and my eyes averted from the TV screen. I explained to her what was happening, and she stood by and watched the TV screen. The ball went up, and Paula began screaming, "It's going wide, it's going wide. He missed, he missed!" I looked up, and saw the ball drift wide of the crossbar. He missed! The game was not over; my Vikings still had a chance!

It turns out that the broadcasters were replaying Gary Anderson's missed field goal from several minutes earlier. Paula was simply unaware that she was seeing the replay. (In retrospect, Paula could have hardly thought of a funnier joke to play on me.) Moments later the Atlanta field goal kicker lined up and smacked the ball right between the uprights, and my Vikings slumped off the field in defeat.

Two years later, the Vikings were heavily favored to crush the New York Giants in the NFC title game. And once again, they failed to make the Super Bowl, this time in a blowout. By the end of the first quarter, it was obvious that the Vikings would lose. My team never had a chance.

Objectively speaking, I ought to feel better about the Atlanta game than the New York game. The Vikings made a respectable showing in the Atlanta game, coming within a field goal of making it to the Super Bowl. In the Giants game, the Vikings were humiliated. But anybody who is a sports fan will know which game has caused me the most angst over the years. The Atlanta game drives me crazy because it is so easy to think of ways that the game could have turned out differently: "If only Gary Anderson had made that field goal. If only Atlanta had not had that lucky break on their third quarter drive. If only, if only. . . ."

All too often, counterfactual thinking only makes us feel worse. Consider two people who sustain spinal cord injuries because of motor vehicle accidents. One man had been traveling along his normal commuter route. The other had decided on the spur of the moment to take an alternative route. Which one do you think will feel worse about his disability? In both cases, it will be easy to think of ways that the accident could have been avoided, perhaps by leav-

ing the house five minutes later. But the person who chose the
unusual route to work is likely to be plagued by "what ifs." "If only
I had driven along my normal route, I could have avoided this
injury."

There are times counterfactual thinking can comfort people by
giving them a sense that bad events happen for a reason. For example, people with spinal cord injuries who blame themselves for their
injuries are generally happier than those who think that their injuries
occurred by chance. A person injured because he drove his car too
fast might be bothered by counterfactual thinking ("if only I had
driven more slowly") but at least he will know *why* the accident happened. He can more easily retain his sense of the world as a logical
place where events happen for reasons. Compare this person to
someone who developed spinal cord paralysis because of a rare and
mysterious disease. This latter person will be plagued by the thought
that the world is full of random, harmful events that he or she has
no ability to control.

In Greg's case, he was stricken by a random, harmful event that
had no simple explanation. But he was not thrown into an existential funk, wondering why the world was full of such inexplicable
cruelty. Instead, his positive attitude arose because all the counterfactual alternatives he thought about were those that made him feel
better about his current situation. He thought about the four times
his heart stopped and realized that he was lucky to be alive. He
thought about the two-and-a-half weeks he'd spent in a coma and
breathed a sigh of relief that he hadn't suffered serious brain damage. If he had never lapsed into a coma and if his heart hadn't
stopped four times, he might have been plagued by regret that the
doctors had not diagnosed him quickly enough to save his legs. But
his narrow escape from death served to focus his counterfactual
thoughts on what would have happened had things gotten even
worse, with the result that he was actually happier than he would
have been if he hadn't been so sick.

Summing It Up

Counterfactual thinking makes people happy when they focus on ways their life could have been worse, just as it makes them unhappy when they obsess about ways they could have turned out better. Hence those paradoxical situations in which people who are worse off in objective terms are actually happier than other people because they focus more of their thoughts on the worse fates they might have experienced. Perhaps this was most brilliantly demonstrated by a team of psychologists led by Victoria Medvec, who studied the words and facial expressions of Olympic athletes after they won either silver or bronze medals. Objectively speaking, silver medalists should be happier than bronze medalists having finished second rather than third. But Medvec discovered that silver medalists were plagued by upward counterfactual thoughts, thinking about the gold medal they almost won, whereas bronze medalists were relieved at having avoided a fourth place finish, which would have left them off the medal stand. When interviewed on television, silver medalists spoke about how they almost won gold, whereas bronze medalists spoke about their happiness at winning a medal. Bronze medalists also had happier facial expressions than silver medalists.

Focused on the terrible fates he had only just narrowly avoided, Greg Hughes was thinking like a bronze medalist, and, consequently, he was not unhappy about his current fate.

Minimizing Emotional Pain with Social Comparison Thinking

Greg's time in the rehabilitation hospital furnished him with ample opportunity to consider just how much worse his fate could have been. Greg was surrounded by people who had suffered recent disabilities. Many of them had less severe disabilities than he did, having only lost one leg or only suffered a below-the-knee amputation. But Greg didn't focus on these people. Instead, he minimized his emotional pain by thinking about all the people in the rehabilitation hospital who were *worse* off than he was—people with spinal cord injuries who had lost the *use* of their legs. "They still have their legs, but they will never walk again," he told me. "With prosthetics I might eventually walk for an hour or two at a time." He also noticed people who were unable to cope emotionally with their disabilities as well as he was, which made him feel even better about his situation. This was a wonderful type of circular reasoning: Greg was happy because he could tell that he was happier than most people.

Clearly, Greg had an intuitive grasp of how to look upon other people in ways that would minimize his pain. He instinctively focused his attention on people around him who were worse off than he was. He did not do this out of spite or pity but rather as a way to feel better about his own situation. Accurately or inaccurately, he selectively interpreted other people's lives in ways that would help him cope with his new disability.

Thomas Cash cleverly demonstrated the subtle ways in which social comparison thinking influences people's moods by giving female college students a series of photographs of women and asking them to make judgments about the people in the pictures—about how attractive, noticeable, and familiar looking they were. Cash gave some students pictures of average-looking women and others pictures of very attractive women. At the end of the picture session, Cash asked students how attractive they felt. Not surprisingly, students exposed to the pictures of attractive women felt less attractive than the other students.

But Cash wasn't done yet. He gave a third group of students pictures of the same attractive women, but in these cases he randomly pasted brand names, like Calvin Klein, into the pictures to hint that these women were professional models. At the end of the picture session, these students were not made to feel unattractive by these pictures. In fact, they felt just as attractive as those students who had been exposed to pictures of average-looking women. They did not think that professional models were a relevant peer group. After all, models are *supposed* to be attractive, so their beauty did not trigger social comparison thinking.

This raises an important question: When people confront adversity, whom do they consider to be relevant peers? As it turns out, people typically compare themselves to others whom they perceive as being worse off than they are. A woman with localized breast cancer will compare herself to someone whose breast cancer has metastasized. A person with a below-the-knee amputation will compare himself to someone with an above-the-knee amputation. People with illness or disability are often so strongly drawn to downward social comparisons, in fact, that when downward social comparisons are not readily available, they construct imaginary patients who are worse off than they are.

But it is rarely necessary to create such imaginary patients because illness and disability often expose patients to people who are worse off than they are. When the acclaimed novelist Reynolds Price was suffering in pain and disability from cancer (he is one of the fifteen hundred people in the United States other than Jay Schreiner who have a chordoma), he spent some time in a rehabilitation hospital. He soon found out that his situation was not nearly as bad as he had originally thought:

> . . . looking back I can see that by far the most important gain of the four weeks came in the intimate day-and-night contact with other people as hard up as I and often much worse. There were some twenty of us, and our range of damage included octogenarians and a young woman-dentist halted by strokes, a woman in late middle age who'd lost a leg to diabetes, an older woman whose breast cancer had moved to her spine and stalled

her legs, a young woman who'd attempted to shoot herself through the heart but had hit her spinal cord, and a young man of Olympian physique whose wife (having caught him in the flagrant act with another woman) shot him through the spine and paralyzed his legs. . . . At the very still core of our tribe was the beautiful child we centered on—our tragic worst, a fourteen-year-old girl whose kid brother had accidentally leapt on her neck at a swimming party in celebration of their father's second marriage. By the time I left rehab, she could turn her head slightly and barely flex her thumbs. Many months later I'd hear she was there still little improved.

My guess is that the comparison thinking worked in both directions—that other patients in the rehabilitation hospital looked upon Reynolds Price as being more unfortunate than *they* were. The woman who had lost her leg from diabetes, for instance, could easily view Price's chordoma as an unimaginable tragedy. Just as the adulterous man with a spinal cord injury probably viewed his relatively stable disability as being much better than Price's progressively crippling tumor.

Being Above Average

While staying in rehabilitation hospitals, Greg Hughes and Reynolds Price perused their surroundings and concluded that they were better off than the majority of patients they encountered. Those other patients perused the same corridor and probably came to the same conclusion. One could almost say that the rehabilitation hospitals like this one become like the fictional town of Lake Wobegon, where *all* the children are above average.

Indeed, the social psychologist Shelley Taylor is convinced that people are happy in part because they have been fooled into thinking that their position in the world is better than it really is. They hold overly positive views of themselves—their abilities, their physical attractiveness, and their overall happiness. Most people rate their work performance as above average; most people with terminal illnesses believe that their own chance of survival will be better than average; and most people rate themselves as above average drivers, even those who have been in multiple automobile accidents. They also hold *unrealistically* optimistic visions of the future. The majority of college students predict they will experience above average job satisfaction after graduation; most married couples believe their chance of becoming divorced is far less than average; and most people are convinced that they have a better than average chance of avoiding alcoholism, cancer, or Alzheimer's disease.

Are We Fooling Ourselves?

How can so many of us be fooled into thinking that we are better than we really are and that we will experience a future devoid of misery? Undoubtedly, our mothers deserve some blame for telling us so many times how extraordinary we are and what a perfect life we would live. But the blame primarily resides in our shabby little brains, which do such a rotten job of storing and analyzing the kind of data that would provide us with more accurate estimates of our position in the world. For example, take the way people rate themselves as drivers. When rating myself, my brain primarily conjures up images of all the rotten drivers I encounter on my daily commute. I think of all the drivers I see violating one traffic law or another, and it feels like the world is teeming with rotten drivers. In such a world, how could I *not* be a better than average driver? However, in evaluating my driving ability, I forget to consider the hundreds or thousands of other drivers I encounter who do not violate any laws and who, in fact, might be driving more carefully than I (probably because they are not obsessively looking around at other drivers to see if they are breaking any laws). I overestimate my driving ability because my recollection of other people's driving behavior is skewed—I selectively remember people who are worse drivers than me because bad driving is more memorable than good (and thus boring) driving.

Selective memories also contribute to positive self-illusions because people do not like thinking about bad experiences. Consequently, when asked to think about whether their life is made up of generally good or bad experiences, the good experiences come to mind more easily, thereby distorting their self-assessments. I make this mistake sometimes when mentoring new researchers. I wonder why it takes them so long to write manuscripts or why their grant proposals sometimes get rejected, forgetting that when I was at their stage, it took me even longer to write papers and my grants were routinely rejected. I have simply blocked all the pain out of my mind, leaving me with an overly rosy view of my early career.

Selective interpretation plays an important role in positive self-illusions, too. I was embarrassed by such an interpretation once in high school when (for purposes that have escaped me) our teachers told us to fill out self-assessment questionnaires. My friend John Hough looked over my shoulder and saw that I had rated my athletic ability as being "in the top 5 percent of the class." He broke out laughing. He was a football quarterback and a hockey standout, while I was a 135-pound weakling who played sports that had lower social standing, like soccer and basketball. (Basketball gets *no* respect in Minnesota!) By his standards, I was nowhere near the top 5 percent of the class. But I was using different standards to judge my athletic ability from those John was using. I interpreted athletic ability to mean quickness and hand-eye coordination and ignored my inability to survive a single bone-crushing tackle on the gridiron. Cross-country runners, whom we soccer and basketball players thought of as uncoordinated automatons, no doubt interpreted athletic ability to mean endurance and stamina. The power forward on the basketball team probably thought about how few other people in the class could dunk a basketball. By our own internal measures, many more than 5 percent of us thought of ourselves as being in the top 5 percent of the class. And by our own internal measures, we were. We were all simply choosing the standards by which our own athletic abilities would be most highly rated.

The same phenomenon likely explains why most people consider themselves to be happier than average. Some people think of themselves as happier than average because they recognize that they are in good moods more often than other people. Others, who are less frequently in good moods, consider themselves happy because they are pursuing more important and meaningful goals than others. Perhaps happiness, like athletic ability, is a vague enough notion that it is theoretically possible that most of us are happier than average.

My sports analogy reveals another powerful tendency that enables people to have positive views of themselves: we choose to pursue the things we excel in. I chose not to play high school football because my chance of excelling at football was significantly lower than my chance at excelling in other sports (and also in large part because my mother would not let me play). People often choose sports, college majors, and careers based on their specific strengths. I think visual arts are fascinating, for example, but I cannot draw a straight line to save my life. It should not be surprising that my college art career was limited to a pass/fail art history course. Most people gravitate to things that they do relatively well. Consequently, they feel better about their abilities. Finding what they do best is part of what makes people happy.

People also develop unrealistically positive views of themselves by selectively interpreting information about themselves, usually so they come out looking better than they would without such selectivity. When they get good feedback from someone, they wholeheartedly embrace the comments. When they receive negative feedback, they find ways to discount the opinion. When they feel that they will fail in a situation, they behave in a way that invites failure, thereby providing a ready-made excuse for failure that does not threaten their self-esteem. If I waited until the very last minute to ask a girl out for a Saturday night date in high school, then I wouldn't have to blame the inevitable rejection on how unattractive I was. Most of us view the world through rose-tinted glasses. In normal times, this slightly distorted view allows us to believe we are better than we really are. When we experience adversity, it enables us to hold on to our self-esteem and helps us find a way of convincing ourselves that things aren't as bad as they seem.

Is It Always Good to Be Above Average?

Greg Hughes developed a positive attitude about his disability in part because he convinced himself—by looking around at other patients in the rehabilitation hospital—that his disability was not so bad. Like most of us, Greg Hughes liked to believe he was above average. But that didn't mean he wanted to spend time hanging out with people he believed to be below average. People do not necessarily choose to spend time with the people who would make them feel above average. In fact, when psychologists Vicki Helgeson and Shelley Taylor interviewed cancer patients, they discovered that most of them wanted to *think about* those cancer patients who were worse off than they were while actually *spending time* with those who were better off. They especially preferred spending time with patients who used to be in their position but who were now better off— patients who had been cured by chemotherapy or who had survived a bone marrow transplant. These patients gave them hope that their cancers, too, would be cured. By contrast, they didn't want to spend time with people whose cancers had metastasized because doing so made them worry that their cancers would metastasize, too.

As should be clear by now, the relationship between social comparisons and happiness is a tricky one, forcing people to hang out with one group of people (whom they try not to compare themselves to) while comparing themselves to another group of people (whom they prefer to avoid). However, the relationship is even trickier than I have let on. Downward social comparisons, for example, do not always make people happy. For example, 1980s research showed that HIV-infected people who had not developed AIDS (the disease that results when the HIV virus has weakened the immune system) became miserable when they made downward comparisons to people with AIDS. They became miserable because such comparisons reminded them of their own destiny since HIV infection was essentially untreatable at the time. Downward comparisons do not lift people's spirits when people believe they are heading downward. They only lift people's spirits when they believe they will remain better off than the people they compare themselves to.

The key here is that the effect of downward comparisons on people's moods depends on their beliefs. If an HIV patient in the 1980s believed strongly enough that he or she would avoid becoming sick, then thinking about people with AIDS would not necessarily make him or her miserable.

Sometimes downward comparisons lift people's moods and other times they depress their moods; sometimes people should hang out with people who are better off than they are, and other times they should not; and they should be ready to shift around the kind of social comparisons they make if their circumstances reduce their level of unrealistic optimism. So, how do individuals know which social comparisons that they should dwell upon, in order to find happiness?

I can tell you one thing—they don't sit around reading social psychology studies and analyzing their social comparison options. Instead, people let their emotions guide their thinking. When they feel rotten, they try to find ways to feel better. People find happiness through trial and error. If thinking about something makes them unhappy, they try to think about something else.

The Evolutionary Advantages of Happiness

Whether experiencing good or bad circumstances, people tend to be happy. Not necessarily ecstatically, bouncing off the wall happy, but happy enough that the frequency and intensity of their good moods outweigh that of their bad moods. Which raises the question: Why are so many people so happy so much of the time? Scientists are increasingly convinced they have a good answer to this question. They blame it all on evolution.

For a long time, psychologists ignored evolution. Behavioral psychologists, like Ivan Pavlov, made their dogs salivate in response to various environmental stimuli. In an effort to make psychology rigorous, similar to chemistry and physics, they abandoned any concern about *why* animals think or feel the way they do in favor of concerning themselves with outwardly visible, objective, and reproducible behaviors. Measuring thoughts and feelings was too messy and hardly trustworthy enough to elevate psychology into the elite company of the natural sciences. Behaviorists studying anger wouldn't study anger per se but would study the external manifestations of what a layperson would call anger. Poke and prod a dog with a stick, and it would bare its teeth and growl—an observable behavior. Prod it some more, and it might attack. A behaviorist would be content to study the circumstances under which dogs, rats, or, on very rare occasions, humans would exhibit specific behaviors, without trying to figure out why they behaved that way.

At its extreme, this approach is atheoretical—behaviorists don't develop theories about why dogs become angry after they are poked and prodded but simply tabulate which stimuli produce which responses. But true understanding requires a higher level of understanding. We might know that a poke in the eye produces a stronger reaction than a poke in the ribs. But we want to know why. Is it possible that the eye poke causes more pain? Moving to a higher level of theorizing, we might wonder whether pain is an important signal to alert animals to protect themselves. Moving up a notch higher, we might even figure out that animals that perceive and respond to pain have survival advantages over those that do not.

Evolution is the key to understanding biology. And the brain, the seat of thinking and feeling, is as much a product of evolution as any other bodily organ. Thoughts and emotions—and the manner in which external stimuli lead to these emotions—evolved. It follows, then, that human beings are biologically programmed to feel things like anger, joy, lust, and jealousy in order to reproduce their genes and that common behaviors or emotions probably became common because they created survival advantages for those organisms experiencing them. Slap a sea urchin and it does not get angry. Anger evolved in some organisms because it brought survival advantages to these organisms.

The Advantages of Moods

The evolutionary benefits of negative moods have always been easy to appreciate. Negative emotions focus people on specific behaviors. Fear makes people want to escape, hunger makes people want to eat, and disgust makes people want to throw up. These emotions have clear evolutionary functions. Fear motivates people to run away from life-threatening situations, anger provides them with the strength and resolve to fight back when escape is not possible, and disgust encourages people to avoid ingesting foods that could potentially harm them.

Each of these negative emotions does its job by narrowing people's attention, focusing people's disgust, fear, or anger at some specific thing. In fact, when people can't figure out why they are disgusted, afraid, or angry, they usually focus their mental energy on looking for the source of their emotion. People can be afraid because a foreboding stranger is approaching them suspiciously or because they are in a dark alley alone; in either case, you can be assured that their neck hairs are standing up on end and they are working very hard to think of ways to avoid danger.

Now imagine walking down that same alley in the middle of the day after having a promising first date with someone you have always hoped to get to know better. You are in a good mood because of the date but your mood is not directed *at* the date. Your good mood is not focusing your attention, say, on looking to see if your lunch companion is about to jump out at you from behind a dumpster to give you a kiss. And even though your good mood might focus your thoughts on your successful lunch date—on the brilliant comments you made that impressed your companion or on the big blue eyes staring at you from across the table—it could just as easily cause your thoughts to wander, to get you thinking that you are finally ready to start that ambitious new work project or that you need to call your parents to tell them you love them. Instead of being focused narrowly on the lunch date, your attention has opened up. You are ready to take on the world.

As it turns out, good moods bring survival advantages, too. People in good moods demonstrate greater flexibility and creativity in their thinking than people in neutral moods or bad moods. When people are in good moods, they have increased attention spans, better memories, and are more likely to seek variety in the choices that they make.

In contrast to negative emotions, positive emotions are much less specific in how they motivate people's behavior. Emotions such as joy, contentment, and a sense of well-being don't usually promote specific activities. Instead, they influence people's general engagement with the world. Positive emotions broaden people's interests, making them better at solving problems and more likely to forge and maintain relationships. When researchers induce good moods in people, they find that people become more interested in their surroundings. Ask people: "What would you like to do right now?" Those who are in experimentally induced good moods will have lots of answers, while those in experimentally induced bad moods will not feel like doing much of anything.

More Advantages of Good Moods

Psychologists and evolutionary theorists have long recognized some of the evolutionary advantages of some types of positive emotion. They have recognized, for example, that good food makes people happy, which makes them more inclined to eat enough calories to survive. They have acknowledged that successful lunch dates make people happy, which make them more inclined to go out on follow-up dates, which eventually can lead to some of the most evolutionarily advantageous behavior ever invented. (I hope I don't have to spell this out for you!) But scientists have only recently recognized the more general evolutionary benefits of good moods.

Good moods, as we have seen, lead to flexible and creative thinking, with a good attention span, a reliable memory, and a willingness to engage one's environment. Sounds like a winning evolutionary combination to me! Imagine two cavemen who have hunted unsuccessfully for three days in a row. The happy caveman does not give up, convinced that the next day will bring him food. The unhappy one gives up, retreating into his cave to bemoan his bad luck. Unrealistic optimism, with a pinch of self-illusion ("I'm better at finding food than other people") will provoke the happy caveman to keep looking for food until he eventually finds the food. What's more, his happy mood will induce the kind of open-minded creative thinking that will increase his chance of finding food. ("Hey, what if I kill an animal with a rock so I can eat the animal!") Furthermore, happy and extraverted people generally have larger social networks than unhappy introverts do. So, the happy caveman might survive even if he is unsuccessful at hunting because he has friends who are willing to share their meat with him. It can pay off to be a happy caveman!

Happiness pays off so well, in fact, that good moods even help people live longer. Now there is an evolutionary advantage! A striking piece of evidence for this phenomenon comes from an analysis of essays written in the 1930s by novice nuns. Researchers analyzing the essays found out that those nuns who expressed more positive emotions in their essays lived longer than other nuns did. And their longevity could not be attributed to different lifestyles since all the nuns refrained from cigarettes, alcohol, and other health hazards. Instead, those nuns lived longer primarily because they were happier than other nuns.

Studies of emotions and the immune system offer one possible explanation for this longevity. Levels of immunoglobin A rise and fall according to experimentally induced moods. People in bad moods have weaker immune systems. When people experience negative events in their lives, they are more prone to cold viruses. In fact, when researchers have exposed people to cold viruses on purpose by having them breathe in infected air particles, they can predict who is most likely to come down with a cold by measuring their emotions at the time of the exposure. Being happy is good medicine.

The Risks of Rose-Colored Glasses

Happiness is pervasive, and some portion of this pervasiveness results from illusory thinking. People hold unrealistically rosy views of themselves or their futures and, consequently, fool themselves into being happy. But is this kind of illusory thinking safe? Misperceiving the world can be risky. After all, rose-colored glasses may give people a rosy outlook on life, but they also make it difficult for people to see properly. By the same token, unrealistic thinking, even if it makes people happy, also distorts people's perceptions of reality, and these distortions could have disastrous consequences.

In my clinical practice, I have encountered patients who reject beneficial therapies because they believe they can beat their illnesses alone. Are these illusions doing people any good? Cancer patients are typically referred to hospices in the last few days of their lives, rather than earlier in their illnesses when they could benefit more from hospice care. Could unrealistic optimism on the part of patients or doctors be contributing to these late referrals?

At an extreme, positive illusions can be dangerous. When unrealistic optimism convinces a person that he can jump a motorcycle over the Grand Canyon, he will end up in an intensive care unit or a morgue. But most unrealistic thinking is not this extreme, and even when it is extreme, it is rarely harmful. Even though many people have unrealistically positive views of, say, their athletic ability, relatively few abandon their schoolwork to engage in a futile pursuit of an athletic career. Even though most newly diagnosed cancer patients have an unrealistic perception of their survival odds, few ignore their doctors' advice about what treatments to undergo.

Perhaps most illusions are not harmful. But what happens when people realize the wrong-headedness of their beliefs? What happens when they discover they aren't so far above average as they thought?

Protecting Our Optimism

Fortunately, most people are quite good at holding on to their positive illusions, even in the face of clear evidence that they have been fooling themselves. Convinced it will finally bring us happiness, we get a new job but it turns out to be just as boring as our old job. We start a new romantic relationship, convinced we have finally found fulfillment, and find out our new lover is just as obnoxious as the old one. Yet we persist in our optimistic fantasy world. We reinterpret events to protect our optimistic view of the world. We convince ourselves the *next* job and the *next* relationship will work out. Or we forget the high expectations we held before starting that new job or that new romance and never have to admit that our worldview is so inaccurate. I probably would not have written this book if I hadn't fallen prey to unrealistic optimism—visions of Oprah and the *New York Times Book Review* dancing in my head. When Oprah and the *New York Times* shun my book, I will be unhappy but I will quickly convince myself that my real expectation was to write a book that brought pleasure to a few thousand readers, or that my next book will make it to the big time, or that all that really matters is that I enjoyed writing the book.

People's flexibility in interpreting events is nicely demonstrated by the way professional athletes thank God for their athletic victories. You probably know what I am talking about. A football player crashes through the line of scrimmage and leaps into the end zone for a touchdown. He falls on one knee, bows his head, and says a prayer of thanks to God. Does he really think that God took sides in the game and helped him score a touchdown? If he had been stopped at the line of scrimmage, would he have blamed God? Of course not. He would have assumed that it was God's will that he be stopped at the line of scrimmage (God works in mysterious ways after all), or he would not have thought about God's role in the game at all.

This flexibility is not limited to trivial events like football. Take, for example, a person with cancer who is convinced that she can prevent a recurrence through optimism and a macrobiotic lifestyle. What happens to her optimism when the cancer recurs? Many patients in this situation convince themselves that they would have had an even *earlier* recurrence if they had not followed a macrobiotic diet or that their attitude and behavior have improved their quality of life. Some decide that further efforts will cure their recurrence, while others assume that their recurrence is part of God's plan for them. Like Voltaire's Candide, people can experience calamitous circumstances and still convince themselves that everything is working out for the best.

While in the rehabilitation hospital, Greg Hughes was confident that things would turn out for the best. He was already brainstorming about alternative careers that wouldn't be affected by his disability and planning for the day when he could retool his car so he could compete in local races. All the while, his uncle loomed in the back of his mind, the counterfactual social comparison to end all comparisons.

Greg witnessed his uncle's life spiral out of emotional control after the accident. He saw his uncle drinking heavily and arguing with his wife. By Greg's recollection, his uncle became a nasty, messed-up person after his accident.

Is Greg going to become like his beloved uncle, drinking himself into oblivion while his marriage falls apart, the next victim of the Dansville, auto-mechanic, Hughes-family curse? Greg doesn't give this possibility any thought. He knows he has his life in order and is confident that he will cope more effectively with his disability than his uncle did. If anything, he reflects on his uncle's situation to remind himself how *not* to respond to his misfortune. His uncle lives on in his mind not as a sign of his own cursed fate but as a reminder of what could happen to him if he is not careful.

While in the rehabilitation hospital, Greg wasn't purposely setting out to make the kind of counterfactual and social comparison judgments that would make him happy. Instead, these were simply the judgments that came naturally to mind. He was genuinely grateful for avoiding a worse fate. He was delighted that he had not died and that nothing seemed to stand in the way of him continuing to live with the woman he loved.

When people imagine Greg's life, they might focus on his leg amputations. But Greg is convinced that he has a healthier, happier marriage than 90 percent of people will ever enjoy. Think about that, he says, when contemplating what his life is like.

5

Uncertain Resilience

It all began when Scott Mackler's tennis racquet slipped out of his hand a couple of times during our weekly tennis match. I assumed it must have been the force of my ground strokes, but Scott, recognizing that my forehand would barely bruise an overripe banana, assumed the problem lay in his racquet, so he turned it in at the front desk to be regripped.

At the time, Scott was what the University of Pennsylvania calls a "physician-scientist," meaning he took care of patients, conducted research, lectured to medical students, and taught medical residents. He was a busy man. Yet, despite his busy career, Scott always found time for athletics. This is a man, after all, who during his own residency training, while working one hundred hours a week in the hospital, found time to run the Boston Marathon. Twice. Scott's passion for exercise had continued to that day, with Scott taking a break from his lab work each day to either jog or play tennis.

So I was surprised when he cancelled our next two tennis matches; surprised and frustrated because I had been on a total roll lately, slaughtering Scott the last five times we had played ever since he made the fatal mistake of bragging in public about beating me. Was he afraid to lose again? I couldn't wait until the next time I saw Scott when I could razz him about his cowardice.

But I never got a chance to razz him. The next time I saw him was simply not the right place or time to give him such grief. It was a business dinner, at which we were trying to recruit to the Penn faculty a researcher who shared Scott's commitment to helping patients overcome chemical dependency. Although I didn't get a chance to razz Scott that evening, the night was still memorable to me in large part because it was my first chance to spend extended time with Scott's wife, Lynn, who can only be described as a force of nature. Lynn is a physical therapist, internationally recognized for her research on knee injuries. Similar to Scott, she was intense about work and play, a scholar/jock par excellence. But unlike Scott, she struck me as lacking charm—all intensity, no sense of humor. While Scott was always quick to laugh and joke, Lynn seemed humorless. She was a great researcher and probably a compassionate clinician but not someone you'd want to share a cocktail hour with.

First Impressions Can Be Misleading

A few days after the dinner, I learned how wrong I had been about Lynn's humorlessness and about Scott's cowardice. I was walking across campus with Scott after a meeting, and he told me the real reason he had not been able to play tennis. "Peter," he said, "I have fasciculations." The magnitude of Scott's words did not sink in right away so, a couple of strides later, he repeated them more forcefully. "Peter . . . I have fasciculations!"

Fasciculations are involuntary muscle contractions in which tiny muscle groups fire in small, continuous rippling motions, with barely enough strength to move the overlying skin. When Scott showed me his forearm, it looked like his arm muscles were doing the wave right under his skin. Fasciculations are much weaker than the contractions that cause Parkinson's tremors or the kind of hereditary tremors that Katharine Hepburn had. But despite their weakness, fasciculations are far more devastating than these stronger tremors, because they are an almost sure sign that someone is developing amyotrophic lateral sclerosis (ALS), better known as Lou Gehrig's disease. So when Scott said, "Peter, I have fasciculations," he was really telling me, "Peter, I think I have ALS. Every skeletal muscle in my body, from the muscles that raise my eyebrows to those that wiggle my toes, is going to die. The barely discernable weakness in my backhand and the little muscle flutterings in my arm and leg muscles are going to progress relentlessly until I will no longer be able to swallow food, or walk across campus, or lift up my arms to wipe my nose."

I was overwhelmed by the telltale ripplings taking place under Scott's shirt sleeve. I was overwhelmed with guilt, for thinking that Scott was a coward, for believing that his wife was humorless, and for overlooking, completely overlooking, that Scott had looked out of sorts at dinner that night. I had spent the evening completely unaware that Scott and Lynn were consumed by anxiety over Scott's health. Mainly, though, I was just overwhelmed by shock, in total disbelief that Scott might have ALS.

If Scott had told me he had cancer, I would have been shocked and devastated, but I would have also probably wondered what kind of cancer it was and how far it had spread and what treatments there were. Cancer is almost always treated surgically or medically, leaving hope to most people, at least early on, that it can be cured or slowed. But to me, a diagnosis of ALS meant only one thing—inevitable, inexorable death. There are no effective treatments for ALS. Most people die within five years when their muscles become so weak that they can no longer breathe. Some people die even earlier than that. Lou Gehrig's first symptoms of ALS occurred when he was only thirty-six years old, still in the midst of the longest streak of consecutive games in baseball history. He died less than three years later.

Walking across campus that day, I couldn't believe my friend was dying. Those fasciculations couldn't be real. They couldn't be a result of ALS. This couldn't be happening.

Dealing with Uncertainty

Walk into a dimly lit room, and your pupils will immediately dilate. In less than one minute, you will begin to see objects clearly again. Catch a cold virus, and your immune system will begin mobilizing its resources within hours; in less than a week, you will probably feel healthy again. But experience a significant new illness or disability and your emotions are not likely to recover as quickly as your vision, and your psychologic immune system will probably require more than a week or two to allow you to feel happy again. Some people, like Greg Hughes, shrug off misfortune as quickly as if it were a minor cold virus. But most people do not recover so quickly.

The first few months after experiencing fasciculations, Scott and I started meeting for lunch because we could no longer play our weekly tennis match. Scott hadn't told many people about his symptoms so he needed someone to talk to. I was struck at how tired he looked; the brightness had left his eyes, replaced by dark circles. He told me he was having a hard time sleeping, tossing in bed consumed with anxiety about what was happening. I told him he looked great.

Scott's first fasciculations occurred in December 1998, when he was only forty-two years old. But this was not the first time he had worried about his neurologic health. A decade earlier, Scott had experienced unusual neurologic symptoms in his right arm, slightly reminiscent of, but not identical to, the fasciculations he was currently experiencing. These symptoms went away as mysteriously as they had appeared. But now, Scott was experiencing arm symptoms again, and he wondered whether his new symptoms would go away, too. Wishful thinking, he realized, because these symptoms were more ominous. This time, his muscles were fasciculating in a way they had not before. And this time, Scott was starting to feel some weakness in his hands, another symptom he had not experienced previously. As much as he hoped these symptoms would go away,

Scott was pretty sure they would not. Pretty sure, but not definitely sure, and that tiny bit of uncertainty would torture Scott over the next few months.

Several weeks after experiencing these new fasciculations, Scott went to see a neurologist, hoping to learn the differential diagnosis of his symptoms—he wanted to know what could be causing his fasciculations. Actually, he wanted to know what else besides ALS could be causing them. But the neurologist would not discuss Scott's differential diagnosis, even refusing to tell Scott that his symptoms might be due to ALS. I ate lunch with Scott several days after his neurology appointment, and he was still angry at his neurologist: "*I* knew ALS could cause my symptoms, and *he* knew that it could cause my symptoms," he told me, "so why wouldn't he even mention it?" Scott was irate at his neurologist's incommunicativeness, which had served only to augment the uncertainty of his whole situation. He lay in bed at night, unable to sleep, fearing that he had ALS but not really knowing whether he had it.

I wondered whether Scott was simply in the early stages of dealing with his illness. Bestselling author Elizabeth Kubler-Ross has famously described the five stages of death and dying: denial ("No, not me; it cannot be true"), anger, bargaining ("If you get rid of my ALS, I will go to church every week"), depression, and, finally, for those who manage to overcome depression, acceptance. Although Kubler-Ross acknowledges that people sometimes go back and forth across these stages, she usually describes the stages as if they were inevitable and universal—a set of orderly responses to tragedy, writing in a typical paragraph that, "When the first stage of denial cannot be maintained any longer, it is replaced by feelings of anger, rage, envy, and resentment." I figured Scott needed time to proceed through these five stages.

But how much time would Scott need? In those first few months, it didn't look to me like he was proceeding through any orderly kind of coping process, and he appeared to be nowhere close to accepting his fate. In fact, he hadn't even reached the stage of denial but seemed to be stuck in a state of bewilderment, unable to deny, bemoan, or accept his fate because he was still uncertain about what his fate would be. Scott was experiencing fasciculations, but he had not received a definitive diagnosis of ALS. I expect it would have been hard for Scott to learn from his neurologist that he had ALS. Even though Scott was already convinced he had the disease, a definitive diagnosis would probably have eradicated any doubts lingering in his subconscious. But what was it like to go to a neurologist and *not* receive a diagnosis?

The Science of Uncertainty

In his midthirties, Woody Guthrie, already famous for composing *This Land Is Your Land,* was feeling restless and behaving erratically. He attributed his behavior to alcohol and venereal disease, punishment perhaps for his promiscuous lifestyle. He didn't want to believe that he had inherited his mother's problems. His mother, Nora, had struggled with mental illness for many years before being diagnosed with Huntington's disease shortly before her death in 1930 at age forty-two.

Huntington's disease is a horrific hereditary illness. It generally doesn't cause problems until people reach adulthood, at which point, sometime between ages twenty and fifty, it starts wreaking havoc on people's central nervous system, causing dementia, mental illness, and uncontrollable muscle spasms. The spasms are not constant, like the tremors of Parkinson's disease, nor subtle, like the fasciculations of ALS. Instead, they cause people's arms and legs to move sporadically in a strange serpentine manner as if people are trying to writhe their way into undersized pantyhose or gloves.

Huntington's is an autosomal dominant illness, which means that children have a 50 percent chance of inheriting the disease from a sick parent. Woody Guthrie was in that unlucky 50 percent, and as he toured the country singing folk songs, his disease progressed relentlessly. Even in his sober moments, his unusual muscle movements and his increasing difficulty walking in a straight line led many people to believe he was drunk. He was frequently disoriented and often combative; his first two marriages ended in divorce. He spent the last few years of his life in and out of hospitals, finally succumbing to the illness at age fifty-five.

At the time Nora lived, experts knew almost nothing about Huntington's disease, and it was unlikely that Nora was plagued with uncertainty about whether she had inherited the disease. By the time Woody grew up, in the 1920s and 1930s, physicians had learned that Huntington's was autosomal dominant but hadn't found a way to test whether a person had inherited the disease. It can't have been easy for Woody to live knowing that he was a coin flip away from tragedy. As his symptoms arose, he must have worked hard to find ways of denying that they were due to Huntington's.

The uncertainty that Woody faced is now a thing of the past for many children who stand to inherit Huntington's disease because scientists have developed a test for the Huntington's gene. But is this genetic test a godsend or a curse? After all, what happens when people find out they have inherited the gene? Could anything be worse than knowing you will die a horrible prolonged neurologic death? Rationally speaking, it should be easier to live with a 50 percent chance of Huntington's disease than with a 100 percent chance.

As it turns out, however, people who learn that they inherited the gene are usually happier than those living in genetic limbo. Once people learn that they have the gene, and that they will definitely experience Huntington's, they begin to adapt to their fate. Those who don't know their fates are plagued by uncertainty, not knowing what to expect for themselves or their children, not knowing, for that matter, whether they should even risk having children.

Uncertainty's Stress

Uncertainty is a huge obstacle to emotional resilience. In the 1980s when HIV infection was a death sentence, a survey showed that men were happier after they received HIV test results than while they were waiting for the results, *no matter what their test results revealed!* The uncertainty of not knowing their HIV status was harder to cope with than the certainty of a rapid demise.

Most people have an almost instinctive aversion to uncertainty. This aversion was cleverly demonstrated in a 1961 paper written by Daniel Ellsberg, a RAND researcher who later became famous for leaking the Pentagon papers to the *New York Times*. Ellsberg asked people to imagine that they were standing in front of two urns, each containing a combination of one hundred red and black balls. They could choose a color and grab a ball at random from one of the urns, winning a prize if they chose the correct color. He told them that Urn 1 contained fifty red and fifty black balls, and that Urn 2 contained somewhere between zero and one hundred red balls, with the rest being black.

Suppose you are asked to pick a ball from Urn 1. Which color would you prefer? Unless you had a favorite color, you would be indifferent between the two colors since either color leaves you with a fifty-fifty chance of winning. If asked to choose from Urn 2, you would feel the same way, since the chance of choosing either color is still 50 percent. Now imagine that you are told to choose a color and then to choose an urn. You decide on red and now must decide whether to grab a ball from Urn 1, which has exactly fifty red balls inside, or Urn 2, which might have anywhere from zero to one hundred. Rationally speaking, you should be indifferent between the two urns because your chance of winning is 50 percent with either urn. But most people don't like the extra layer of uncertainty created by the second urn. With the first urn, people know they have a 50 percent chance of winning. But with the second urn, they don't know their actual chance. The urn might have zero red balls in it, leaving them with no chance to win, or it might have one hundred red balls, assuring success. The 50 percent figure feels so much more uncertain with Urn 2, that most people choose Urn 1.

Uncertainty is a very difficult emotion. For example, people living in the suburbs of London during World War II experienced a rash of stomach ulcers in response to the stress of being bombed by German warplanes. And yet Londoners, who were bombed more often, didn't experience stomach ulcers with such frequency. Resolution of this paradox requires an appreciation of the power of uncertainty. People living in Central London were deluged by nightly bombing raids, whereas those living in the suburbs were raided only sporadically. Objectively speaking, it is worse to be bombed nightly than to be bombed less often, bombing being the bad thing that it is. But sporadic bombing *feels* worse because people become so uncertain about when they will be exposed to the next bombing raid.

Human beings are not the only animals susceptible to the stress of uncertainty. When researchers give intermittent shocks to rats, the rats' stress hormones race into overdrive, causing ulcers and immune deficiencies. Because the rats do not know when to expect the next shock, they react the same way that London suburbanites reacted during World War II. However, when researchers sound warning bells before administering shocks to rats, their stress hormones plummet (the rats' stress hormones, not the researchers'). Even though the timing of the shocks is sporadic, the rats learn to relax, as if they think to themselves: "I haven't heard a bell, so I don't need to worry about being shocked."

Controlling Uncertainty

I like to think that knowledge is power and that recognizing the emotional consequences of uncertainty will help people cope with uncertainty. When I encounter friends or patients stressed out by uncertainty, I frequently point out how normal their emotions are, in hopes that they will attribute their stress to uncertainty, thereby experiencing less stress.

But uncertainty is still miserable. Whenever possible, then, it helps to reduce uncertainty. In fact, I made use of this insight a couple of years ago while recovering from surgery to repair torn cartilage in my shoulder.

When the surgeon operated on my shoulder, he tried to tighten it up a bit, to reduce the chance of reinjury. As it turned out, I was quite a prodigy at laying down scar tissue postoperatively, which left my shoulder frozen into place, making it impossible to reach into my back pocket to retrieve my wallet. Unfortunately, the cure for such scarring has not been altered since Medieval times. I would lie on a table, while Dale, my physical therapist and a former marine, grabbed my arm and pulled. Dale would pull my arm sideways, and my shoulder muscles would get pinched between my shoulder socket and the head of my humerus. As he continued pulling my arm, the muscle tissue would get crushed between the opposing bones. Try pinching your bicep with all your strength—it won't begin to approximate the pain. To my utter dismay, Dale informed me that the only way to get over the pinching pain was to pull my arm so hard that my bones no longer abutted each other. So, three times a week, he would pull and pull for what felt like hours while my muscles and nerves screamed in pain—okay, while I screamed in pain—until he either decided I had had enough or until he heard the distinctive popping sound of scar tissue literally being torn apart.

I have never felt anything half as painful as these torture sessions. The first couple of times I underwent this stretching, I ran through my entire vocabulary of profanities. I embarrassed myself, frankly. But then, before the start of my third session on the rack, I figured out how to overcome the pain. I asked Dale to give me a thirty count at the start of each of his stretchings, counting down to zero as he pulled on my arm. Amazingly enough, even though he pulled on me just as hard as before, and even though it hurt just as much, I knew when the pain was going to end, so it was much easier for me to endure the pain. Occasionally, sadist that he is, Dale would get down to the five-second mark and tell me he wanted to pull for another fifteen seconds, but this didn't bother me. Just knowing that this was coming to an end, and that I could count it down, helped me put up with the sessions. Prior to these counting sessions, he would start pulling on my arm and, within five seconds, I would be screaming in pain, wondering when (and deep down wondering *if*) he'd stop torturing me. I had a difficult time handling even fifteen seconds of such pain. But now, Dale was able to stretch my arm for forty-five to sixty seconds at a time, all because I had found a way to reduce the uncertainty of the situation.

Several weeks after seeing the incommunicative neurologist, Scott began to have communication problems of his own. He started to slur his words. The slurring was quite subtle, and Scott was able to hide it by slowing down his speech. Normally, you see, Scott was what Jerry Seinfeld would have called "a sentence finisher"—his brain moved so fast that he often finished people's sentences for them. (I would have found this to be an irritating trait in someone else, but not in Scott, partly because he usually came up with funnier ways of completing my sentences than I would have.) But now, when Scott spoke at his normal speed, his tongue couldn't keep up, making it sound like he'd had one too many beers.

For a while, Scott wondered if the slurring was caused by fatigue, given how poorly he had been sleeping. But over the next month, his slurring got worse. And he began having trouble keeping up with his jogging pals when they challenged each other to sprints at the end of their runs. Scott's doctors still refused to say he had ALS as none of the diagnostic tests had definitively established the diagnosis. But there was no room for doubt in Scott's mind anymore. At the end of a noontime run, one of his friends mocked him for falling behind during the sprint. Scott countered by mocking his friend for being proud about "outrunning a man with a progressive neurologic disorder." Scott's jogging partners stared back in disbelief. Scott's uncertainty had ended, and he now had five more people he could talk with about his illness.

Around this time, I pulled out my internal medicine textbook to read up on ALS. I was so distraught about Scott's symptoms that I could barely make it through the chapter. But what I read made me even more distraught. As I had remembered from my earlier readings, patients with ALS live for an average of five years, a piece of information that had been floating around my head since Scott got sick. But upon rereading the chapter, I was reminded of a particularly aggressive type of ALS that disproportionately affects muscles involved in speech and swallowing. People with this version of ALS live an average of only eighteen months. I thought back to our last tennis match, four months earlier, and realized that Scott might have only fourteen months to live.

I doubt that Scott needed to refer to a textbook to realize how aggressive his illness was—not simply because he had a nearly photographic memory but because he could feel how quickly this illness was progressing, drawing strength from his muscles on an almost daily basis. As the gravity of his illness sunk in, Scott became nostalgic about his life, telling me how lucky he had been to meet Lynn when he was in college and how blessed he was to have spent a decade and a half with his two teenage boys. "Most people who live into their seventies and eighties can't put together forty years that can match up to my life," he told me one day, simultaneously expressing joy about what a great life he had led while also signaling that he knew that the end was near.

One day at lunch, I pretended not to notice when Scott struggled to swallow a Chinese eggplant dish. He refused to let me pretend, quickly shooting out a question. "What do you think I will need first, Peter, a wheelchair, a feeding tube, or a ventilator?" Now I was the one choking on my food while Scott chuckled at his morbid joke. Scott knew that wheelchairs, feeding tubes, and ventilators were in his future. He harbored no hopes of a cure or a miraculous recovery.

The Kind Side of Predictability

ALS is a cruelly predictable disease but in its cruelty lies a bit of kindness because patients with ALS know what to expect. Scott knew he'd soon be in a wheelchair, so he could begin to imagine what that would entail and prepare himself emotionally for what was coming. If Scott had contracted a less predictable illness, he wouldn't have been able to imagine his future so clearly. Take multiple sclerosis (MS), for example. MS is typically much less aggressive than ALS. In its most common form, it stops and starts, flares and remits, with progressive neurologic damage occurring only during flares. Some patients go for years between flares. Unlike ALS, people with MS do not inevitably end up in wheelchairs, and those who do have usually struggled with MS for a decade or more. Do not get me wrong, MS is often a horrible disease. But it is nowhere near as horrible as ALS. People with MS have every reason to hope that their disease will stop progressing before they become debilitated, a hope not available to those with ALS. And yet, the very hope that MS patients cling to—and the uncertainty about when they will have their next flare—can be emotionally debilitating. Some MS patients experience each disease flare as a brand-new setback.

Some end up feeling like experimental rats, experiencing intermittent shocks without a warning bell.

People's emotional experiences are often tied to how clearly they see their future, a fact that explains several paradoxical phenomena. For example, political revolutions often take place *not* when economic and social conditions are deteriorating, as you'd expect, but when they are improving. People imagine how good their future will be and become restless for this future. Prisoners often experience a similar restlessness as they approach the end of their sentences and begin to imagine life outside prison. As a result, they become more likely to escape the closer they get to their release date!

Consider the emotional well-being of people with complete spinal cord injuries versus those with only partial injuries. When people experience a complete severing of their spinal cord, their future is clear. Those with damage high up in their neck will have quadriplegia while those with lower injuries will have paraplegia. But some spinal cord injuries are incomplete—the spinal cord is injured but not completely severed. In these cases, people can usually expect less disability than if their cord had been completely severed. Early in their recovery, these patients often experience neurologic improvements as the portions of the spinal cord that were not severed begin to recover. People whose legs were totally paralyzed at first might regain some leg strength. This is all for the better except for one thing—these people often have difficulty adapting to their uncertain fates. Should they bother holding out hope for improvement? Or will such hopes merely frustrate them when the hopes are not met? Sad to say, and perhaps due to uncertainty about their futures, people with partial spinal cord injuries are actually *more* likely to commit suicide than those with complete injuries.

Neurologically speaking, Scott was worse off than any person with a spinal cord injury and faced a quicker and more relentless deterioration than the vast majority of MS patients ever face. And yet, as his situation became less uncertain, Scott became progressively happier. The brightness returned to his eyes. His jokes recovered their ubiquity, even if they trickled out of his weakening mouth more slowly than usual.

A couple months after his speech problems began, Scott finally received diagnostic confirmation of his ALS, providing a final nail into the coffin of his uncertainty. With the diagnosis now official, he decided to let everyone in on the secret he'd been keeping from them the past six months. So, he composed a message that he e-mailed to friends and colleagues around the world:

> I have a motor-neuron disease and to those of you outside of medicine you will almost certainly know my illness as Lou Gehrig's disease. . . . Before you read through this note that is so hard to write, I ask any of you who could possibly contact Alexander or Noah or my sister or parents to keep this information to yourselves. This includes leaving any messages at home or talking in public places. We will tell our sons in the next week but cannot even yet decide on how to let my parents know.
>
> For the past six months I have noticed a slow but inexorable loss of muscle strength. However, not until last week was the diagnosis official. I have for the entire time realized the nature of this illness, and the final studies only confirmed my suspicions. The uncertainty of three months of watchful waiting amplified the anxiety in our lives. Lynn has been an unbelievable source of support but there is only so much any person can do. There have been so many instances where I have fumbled things in my hands or, more recently, spoken with slurred words. Thankfully, none of you have even mentioned these minor but embarrassing moments to me. To the several friends and colleagues reading this message in whom we have already confided, thank you so much. We will never be able to tell you how much your thoughts have meant to us.

From very early on, Scott showed amazing emotional resilience. He was never in denial. In fact, Scott was living proof of the flaws in Kubler-Ross's view of how people confront death and dying. In her writings, Kubler-Ross made it sound like the five stages were inevitable and universal but few experts in this field agree with that view anymore. Indeed, Scott never was in denial and never became angry. He didn't bargain with anyone and he never became depressed.

Moreover, Scott never allowed himself to be overwhelmed by the uncertainty of his situation. True, his initial emotional reaction to his illness was complicated by feelings of uncertainty. Who wouldn't wonder what is happening to their bodies under such circumstances? Who wouldn't feel, even fleetingly, that this must be a bad nightmare that had to end soon? But his reaction to uncertainty was far less profound than most people's would have been. As we have seen, uncertainty is extremely traumatic for most people, making it difficult for them to summon their emotional resilience. But Scott was more attuned to uncertainty than most people. As an expert clinician, he knew that most medical diagnoses are not 100 percent certain, especially early on in the trajectory of an illness. He could also draw upon enough clinical experience to resolve most of the uncertainty remaining about his diagnosis. On the day he told me that he had fasciculations, he was already aware that he probably had ALS.

With Scott's experience in mind, I try to arm my patients with the kind of knowledge that will help them deal with their situations. Whenever possible, I give them clear and unambiguous information about their illnesses. When their diagnoses are uncertain, I try to give them a sense of what kind of diagnoses they may have, and what I will do to try to resolve the uncertainty. I try to be explicit with them about how hard it can be to deal with such uncertainty, so that they recognize the source of their own feelings and have a chance, therefore, to deal with those feelings.

Just a few decades ago, it was common practice in the United States for doctors to withhold cancer diagnoses from their patients out of concern that the patients would not be able to emotionally handle such information. This practice has largely been abandoned in the United States, a shift that is clearly for the better. Because the opposite is more often true. Uncertainty is harder to live with than even the worst news.

6

The Social Side of Adversity

At some point in our lives, most of us will face serious adversity. How we respond to such adversity will certainly depend on our internal resources—on whether we are strong-willed or weak and on whether we are genetically predisposed toward optimism or pessimism. Our response will, of course, also depend on what kind of adversity we face—how serious it is and whether it is predictable.

When Scott Mackler became sick, as described in Chapter 5, he was able to draw upon a wealth of internal resources. He was strong-willed by nature. Some would even call him stubborn. He also had an indefatigably sunny disposition. But like anyone experiencing adversity, Scott was not facing it alone. Even before sending out the e-mail announcement, Scott could rely on Lynn to help him think and feel his way through the awful things happening to his body. And he could confide in me and his jogging buddies about fears and concerns that he couldn't express to Lynn.

Following his e-mail, however, Scott's illness became public. Would going public make his life better or worse? Scott left town with his family immediately after sending the e-mail, giving everyone a chance to process the news before seeing him. Scott realized that many friends would be coming forward to express their love and their desire to help him. But he must have also realized that many would look at him with a sadness and pity that he had never experienced before.

Would the benefit of their love outweigh the burden of their pity? Scott was a proud man. Six months into his illness, he knew he could still outrun 90 percent of people his age. And despite the weakness spreading across his body, he knew he was as tough as ever mentally. How would his pride respond when confronted with the pitiful looks he knew awaited him upon his return?

Soon, in fact, Scott realized that his illness would become visible even to strangers. Eventually, people would see him shuffling along, unaware that they were looking at a marathon runner whose heart muscle was probably twice as thick as theirs. They would hear him slurring his words and wonder if he was mentally challenged.

Scott even wondered how his own family would respond as his illness progressed. Lynn had been tremendous so far, but how would she manage in the months or maybe even years to come? Stronger marriages than theirs had been destroyed by lesser circumstances.

When people confront adversity, they draw upon far more than their own internal resources, often turning to family and friends for support. But as I learned watching Scott over the next six months, social support is not always everything it's cracked up to be.

Publicly Ill

With his e-mail, Scott's illness had changed from being a relatively private struggle to a more public one. Prior to sending the e-mail message, Scott had purposely limited the number of people who knew about his illness because he didn't want word of his situation to get to his children or his parents. His father was seriously ill, and he didn't want to burden the family with his own illness until he had received a more definitive diagnosis. Scott was relieved that he no longer needed to worry that his children would find out before he'd had a chance to explain things to them. Concealing his illness from them had conflicted with his gregarious nature. He likes to talk, and when he talks, he likes to say what is on his mind, rarely hiding his opinions or emotions.

Sometime after Scott became sick, I read *Falling Down, Laughing*, the autobiography of David Lander, the actor best known for portraying Squiggy on "Laverne and Shirley." In 1984, while filming *Conan the Barbarian*, Lander came down with what he thought was a bad flu, complete with a case of Hitchcockian-level vertigo. Wobbly and exhausted, he was sent home from the set. But the flu did not abate, and he began to experience weakness. At a party shortly after his return home, he fell down while carrying his one-year-old daughter, Natalie, barely able to summon enough muscle coordination to spare her from serious injury.

Lander soon learned he had multiple sclerosis (MS). He spent the next ten years making sure no one else, other than his wife and doctors, knew about his illness, convinced that no one wanted to hire an actor with MS. He labored to conceal his disability, finding creative ways to avoid scenes that required him to walk up stairs and coming up with a series of excuses (bad back . . . bad case of the flu . . .) when his creative suggestions were rejected. But Lander paid a high price for his secrecy. It was hard to live a hidden life. He withdrew from much of the Hollywood social scene and found himself drifting away from longtime friends.

Eventually, he couldn't hide his illness any longer and told his friend Michael McKean (aka Lenny from "Laverne and Shirley") what he'd been concealing from him for the past decade. McKean respected his privacy but soon the signs of Lander's illness became more obvious, and Lander recognized that it was time to go public with his illness. He arranged to speak at an MS benefit and agreed to let *People* magazine write an exclusive story about his illness. Only then did he realize how alone he and his family had felt for the past few years, socially isolating themselves to help conceal his illness.

Now they were deluged with letters and phone calls, from friends and strangers. "After all these years," he wrote, "it was a relief to be finally talking."

Social Support During Hard Times

Like Lander, Scott Mackler was glad that he had more people to talk with about his situation. Talking was therapeutic for Scott. Interacting with people was good medicine for him, medicine he'd had to ration when most people were unaware of his illness. In fact, Scott's life after his e-mail illustrates an important way that people deal with stress—they look to others for support. Earlier, I discussed some ways that people minimize the stress they feel in response to adversity, engaging in things like social comparison judgments and counterfactual thinking to reinterpret their circumstances. But overcoming stress is rarely accomplished alone. Although it helps for people to find positive ways to reinterpret their circumstances, it helps even more if they have other people around to buffer their stress. In times of war, for example, soldiers turn to each other for support. And those soldiers who have stronger relationships with their platoon mates—those in small, stable platoons—have an easier time coping with battle stress.

Friendships reduce stress in part by giving people a chance to talk through whatever is stressing them out. But friendships can reduce stress even in the absence of conversations. For example, when people are anxious about speaking in public, their stress is significantly reduced when a supportive friend is in the audience, regardless of whether they have a chance to talk to their friend. Just knowing that a friend is nearby improves people's moods.

Humans are not the only primates who benefit from social interaction. Baboons who groom other baboons most frequently—and who are in return groomed by other baboons—have dramatically lower levels of stress hormones circulating in their bloodstream than less social baboons. Put a monkey under stress and his stress hormones will surge if he has no other monkeys nearby. Fill the room with unfamiliar monkeys and his hormones skyrocket. But put him in a room with his monkey friends and his stress hormones plummet. It is difficult to overcome adversity without having friends nearby.

Social support can come in even more concrete forms, as I learned when visiting Greg Hughes at his home in Dansville shortly after he left the hospital. Greg had never experienced the kind of social isolation that Scott had experienced. His hospital travails were well known to the Dansville community, with friends and relatives surrounding his bedside even while he was in the coma. And when he regained consciousness, he was rarely without visitors, with his wife, Ruth, constantly at his side and an impressive number of Dansvillians making the hour-long trek to Ann Arbor to visit him.

Greg continued to receive crucial kinds of social support upon his return home. Shortly after returning home, Greg and Ruth decided to go out to a party on a rainy night. On the way out to their truck, Greg's wheelchair got stuck in the driveway, which had turned to mud in the downpour. Even without legs, Greg was a sizeable man and Ruth, pushing with all her might, discovered that her exertions only made the wheelchair sink deeper into the mud. It took Ruth thirty minutes of struggling before she managed to coerce the wheelchair to cooperate. They both arrived at the party soaking wet, forced to sheepishly explain what had happened.

Greg's friends, led by his brother Jack, decided right away that they needed to help Greg out. That's why, when I arrived at Greg's house a couple of weeks after the party, a handful of burly men were out front, hammering the driveway into shape in preparation for covering it in concrete. I walked past them toward Greg's front door, lemon bundt cake in hand, acutely aware of the frailty of my 150-

pound frame but glad, nevertheless, to witness the kind of support Greg was receiving.

Social relationships help people respond to adversity. The long-term survival of people suffering heart attacks depends, in part, on their social situations, with married people or those with some other type of living companion surviving longer than those who live alone. Social engagement promotes health. It's been proven that people live longer when they have frequent contact with friends and family as well as when they are actively involved in social organizations like book clubs or church groups.

In a number of clinical trials, patients randomly assigned to participate in support groups lived longer than those who were not assigned. Details of these studies are controversial, and more recent studies have not always shown such a survival benefit. But no one disputes another finding established in these trials: people in support groups are *happier* than others. When people become sick, they feel better if they can talk about their illness with other patients.

The Downside of Being a Social Animal

Nevertheless, not everyone benefits from social interactions, and no one benefits from every social interaction. Indeed, illness and disability often create uniquely awful social situations, raising a real possibility that some people would have an easier time adapting to their illness if it weren't for other people. In a touching memoir of her internationally famous endocrinologist father, David, Roni Rabine writes about how he became a pariah after developing amyotrophic lateral sclerosis (ALS). The ALS he developed at the peak of his scientific career began as a limp. For a while he told people he had a disk problem in his back, and they accepted his explanation. But as his symptoms progressed, people began to realize that he did not have a back problem. Like Scott Mackler, David finally told his friends that he had ALS. Almost immediately, a large chunk of his colleagues and friends seemed to disappear. Roni became acutely aware of his social isolation when she joined her parents at a scientific conference.

> As soon as David and Pauline walked into the crowded grand ballroom to register their names, they could feel it. For a fraction of a second, the chatter of the crowd dimmed. People turned, stared, and looked away. . . . As David proceeded toward the registration counter, the crowd parted like the Red Sea to make way for him. But it was a gesture of fear more than courtesy. . . . When my parents stood on the curb waiting for the bus that was to take them to the lecture halls, the rest of the crowd gathered several feet away. When my parents sat down at the dining hall, old friends would file past them without even saying hello.

Friends who used to invite them over for dinner parties stopped doing so and would quickly invent excuses for why they could not come over to the Rabines' house for a dinner party. Most people were not trying to hurt David's feelings. They were simply uncomfortable being near this human time bomb. They could not bear to watch him slowly die.

Scott Mackler faced similar reactions when his illness became public. But he refused to let his friends abandon him. One day when we were sharing lunch, he described an encounter he had just had with one of our colleagues, whom I'll call Katherine. Scott hadn't seen her since sending his e-mail announcement. That morning, he saw her approaching as they were walking in a busy corridor. Katherine gave him an awkward hello and began busying herself with some papers that she was carrying. Scott refused to let her pass him by without talking with him. He stopped her and told her not to feel uncomfortable around him. He went on to say that if she had any questions about his health or about what he was going through, she should feel free to ask them and that if anything was bothering her, she should let him know. Scott repeated this type of exchange with dozens of friends and acquaintances over the following weeks. He knew that if he let people walk by him silently a couple of times, they would slip away from him, developing habits that would only get more established as his disease progressed.

ALS is a particularly difficult disease for other people to handle. Not only is it a death sentence, but it is a progressive disabler. A person with incurable pancreatic cancer might be visibly unchanged for much of her illness, making it easier for friends to speak with her without having to be reminded of her fate. But Scott's speech slurring made it impossible to ignore his illness. In addition, his weakness was progressing rapidly, so people who ran into Scott after not seeing him for a couple weeks were bound to notice some new neurologic deficit. Seeing Scott's illness march through his body was too much for some people to handle.

Any sense of social isolation Scott was feeling because of his illness was only intensified when he began to use a wheelchair. The wheelchair made Scott look even weaker than he was. (Despite being in a wheelchair, for example, Scott still kept exercising on his Nordic Track equipment for several months.) Being in a wheelchair also placed Scott several feet below other people, a disconcerting vantage point for holding a conversation. Some friends responded by sitting down or squatting, so they could hold a levelheaded conversation with Scott. But many other friends never seemed to think of this simple response.

Occasionally Scott's efforts at getting people to acknowledge him failed. One of Scott's work colleagues, I will call him Darren, was so troubled by Scott's illness that he refused to visit Scott in his lab. Darren's love for Scott was never in question. In fact, if he had loved

Scott less, he might have been able to visit him. But he was so distressed to see Scott suffering that he, in effect, increased Scott's suffering. Every time I saw Scott, he would ask me how Darren was doing. Scott's mother was in the room one time when he asked me about Darren, and I explained to her how difficult it was for Darren to visit Scott. She was completely unmoved. "Darren better deal with it, no matter how much it bothers him." I confronted Darren about this one day and asked him to think about what it would feel like if the next time he saw Scott was at Scott's funeral. But Darren's emotions were simply too strong to overcome his own moral sensibilities; he knew he ought to visit Scott but could not force himself to do so.

Dealing with Social Stigmas

Perceptions of social stigma often play a large role in how people respond to adversity. When people receive colostomies, for example, they must adjust to living with a pouch protruding from their abdomen. They must learn to cope with the ickiness of emptying their colostomy bags and with the horror of an occasional colostomy leak. Not a pretty sight. Nevertheless, the vast majority of people handle these issues with aplomb. Like parents changing diapers, many find that colostomies aren't nearly as disgusting as they would have predicted.

What people have a harder time coping with, however, is the idea that other people will learn about their colostomies and shrivel up their noses in disgust. Worried that others will see their pouches bulging under their shirts or terrified that they'll have an accident in public, some people withdraw from friends and family, doing what they can to minimize human contact.

Adversity can be difficult to experience in public. A friend of mine lost his job right before our twentieth college reunion. Unemployment was painful enough on its own, but he knew that going to the reunion and explaining that he was "between jobs" would only make matters worse. Being arrested is also a terrible experience in its own right, but the shame of being arrested clearly adds insult to injury; how else to explain the ubiquity of the perp walk. Some adversities, in fact, are adversities only because of the shame they bring upon people. A disfiguring but painless rash would have no bearing on anyone's happiness if people didn't care about what other people thought of them.

Because of ALS, Scott Mackler faced all sorts of situations that many people would consider to be shames and indignities. To his credit, he rarely dwelled on these matters. Instead, recognizing that people couldn't help but respond the way they did, he confronted them and tried to help them overcome their discomfort. He knew that his friends would only become more important as he got sicker.

What Happens When People Can No Longer Be Social?

It is difficult to imagine a situation that would cause Scott Mackler to become withdrawn. But circumstances were conspiring against him, making it increasingly difficult for him to communicate with people. One year into his illness, his speech slurring had progressed to the point where only family members and close friends could understand him. Within a few more months, his sons retained a peculiar ability to understand him, but almost no one else did. Then, I'm so sad to say, he became too weak to speak at all. Never again would I hear Scott's voice.

But this doesn't mean Scott was finished communicating. He still had enough facial strength to smile, glare, roll his eyes, or send a knowing glance in my direction when I made some kind of inside joke. More important, he could still "talk" through his computer. His hands were too weak to use the computer keyboard because the weight of his wrists would press random keys by mistake. But using his mouse, he could direct the cursor over a faux keyboard lit up on his computer screen. He would drag the cursor to the appropriate letter and click. Another computer program would then suggest common words beginning with whichever letter he clicked on. He might type "N" and have the words "no, never, and Nordic" show up. If he wanted to use one of these words, he would drag the cursor to it. If not, he would type in the next letter and receive another series of word choices. Through the miracles of modern technology, Scott could e-mail his friends or, when encountering them face to face, talk with those who were patient enough to wait for him to type out his part of the conversation.

But still, his disease marched along, and with its progression Scott's communication problems increased. As his hands got weaker, it became increasingly difficult to click the computer mouse. Scott overcame this problem by tweaking his word-guessing program so that when he dragged the cursor to a letter and lingered for more than one-and-a-half seconds, the program would select the letter for him. But Scott's muscles continued to weaken. His mousing speed was declining rapidly. It was hard to imagine that Scott would be able to use his computer much longer. How would anyone talk to Scott then? Scott had begun communicating with his family using a code involving his eyebrows and teeth. One click of his teeth signaled a consonant between B and H, which could only be determined by marching through the consonants until Scott looked at you approvingly: "b, c, d . . . Okay, d; what's the next letter. . . ." As laborious as the method sounds, his family and close friends have become quite expert at communicating with Scott this way.

Struggling to Communicate

How important is it to be able to communicate with other people? As Scott's computer skills declined, I found myself envying Christopher Reeve, the actor who used to play Superman, who had developed quadriplegia after falling from a horse. At the time, Reeve could not move his legs or his arms and required a ventilator to breathe. But Reeve could talk, almost normally even, except for the rhythmic intrusion of his ventilated breaths. What I would have given at this point to change Scott's diagnosis from ALS to quadriplegia!

Despite the progression of his illness, Scott still remained in good humor. He still had enough facial strength to smile and enough respiratory musculature to laugh, although he often choked on his own juices each time he heard a bad joke. Occasionally he would type out a bad joke of his own on his computer screen and start laughing and choking, at which point someone in his lab would tell him that he "deserved to choke to death on that joke," leading to more laughter and more coughing, and making me think back to the last time I needed to resuscitate a patient, which had been many years ago. I told him, "Scott, if you choke to death on a bad joke, I will kill you."

But good humor would not stave off the day that Scott would lose the hand strength to operate his computer. He was reaching the point where he would no longer be able to carry on a meaningful conversation with anyone unfamiliar with his eyebrow code. Scott's brain was as sharp as ever—ALS does not affect people's thinking abilities. Scott would still be able to read and watch TV, and his family would still be able to talk with him. But he would not be able to talk back easily. That was a life Scott was unwilling to live. While his hand still had strength, Scott e-mailed his primary care physician and told him that he did not want to be put on a ventilator if he was no longer able to communicate effectively with his family.

Scott was not suicidal or depressed. He had lots to live for and was eager to see his two boys grow up. But he recognized that it would be torture to merely view his surroundings passively. Watching his two boys grow up without being able to communicate with them would be unbearable.

Stubbornly refusing to give in to his disease, Scott began experimenting with a series of devices that would allow him to control his computer with his eyes. The theory of these devices is simple: ALS often spares the extraocular muscles that move the eyes left, right, up, and down. If one of the devices could track Scott's eye movements, then it could follow his commands. Scott tried three different devices. But none of them worked. He learned about a German-made device that responded to electrical impulses produced by the brain, allowing its users to manipulate a computer with their thoughts. But the device was horribly slow and often inaccurate. Scott did not even bother trying it out.

Finally, he tried an optical device called VisionKey. The device was about three inches long and resembled a microscope lens. It was attached to a pair of eyeglasses, sticking out in front of Scott's right eye, leaving his left eye available for normal viewing. Hooked up to this contraption, Scott looked like a Borg with quadriplegia. Peering into the device, Scott could see a grid of letters and symbols. When he focused on a particular part of the grid for a couple seconds, the computer typed in the corresponding letter or symbol. His word recognition program then responded by guessing what word he was trying to spell. If the word he wanted was on the list, Scott gazed at the corresponding number on the VisionKey grid and the computer typed out that word. This was an arduous process, full of stops and starts as Scott told the program to move backward when it typed the wrong letter or word, or as he asked it to execute more complicated commands like "check my e-mail." In the time it takes most people to read this paragraph, Scott could type out five words—if everything was working smoothly.

Because of how slow it was, the VisionKey program created a social dilemma. Should people wait patiently while Scott typed out words or guess what he is saying before he finished? The first time I visited Scott after he began using the device, I jumped ahead and finished one of his sentences. In response, Scott cued a command he had programmed into his computer, causing a box to pop up on his screen telling me to "quit interrupting!" But there were a few people who Scott gladly let interrupt him, like his friend Mark who, being a sentence finisher like Scott, had been in the habit of interrupting Scott even before he became sick. I got to know Mark after Scott got sick and never got to see the two of them interact when both were in sentence-finishing mode. I would love to have seen one of their conversations back then. I envision Scott starting a sentence, Mark chiming in to finish the sentence, and Scott jumping back in to finish the finishing.

Scott's sentence-finishing days were clearly over, but thankfully his sentence starting days were not. Because of modern technology, Scott was still able to communicate with friends, however slowly. For someone as socially active as Scott, someone who had always felt a deep need to interact with people, this ability was the difference between life and death.

What Makes a Nightmare

Early in Scott's illness I dreamt one night that I had just been diagnosed with ALS. Unaware that I was dreaming, I felt overwhelmed with disbelief, horror, and dread. At the center of my emotional pain that night were thoughts about my two sons, then one-and-a-half years and minus four months old, respectively. I was despondent that neither would ever remember me wrestling with them. I ached at the thought that I would never see them grow up and never shape them, or pretend to shape them, into the wonderful adults I knew they would become. Even though it was just a dream, the thought of dying before really getting to know my boys . . . this was the saddest, most painful emotion I had ever felt in my life. I am not the most emotional person in the world, but when I woke up from my dream that night, I was crying.

Prior to this dream, the saddest feelings I had ever experienced occurred six years earlier when I nearly drowned while white-water canoeing in class IV rapids in rural West Virginia. I had gone over a dam and gotten caught in a current flow called a hydraulic. The water was pouring over the top of the dam, curling underneath and spinning back, slowly pulling me toward the dam despite my best efforts. I found myself suspended in the middle of a raging river, unable to swim myself out of the situation because of the strength of the hydraulic. For five minutes, I struggled to stay afloat. But eventually, I started taking water into my lungs and I realized I was going to die. I wondered where they would find my body. I scolded myself for voluntarily taking a canoe down an angry river as if it were an amusement park ride. But mostly, I was sad, incredibly, awfully sad, knowing that within a couple minutes I would be dead, never again to have a sentient thought. It was over. I was over.

My friend George was canoeing with me at the time and was also caught in the hydraulic. We yelled to each other a couple times but were drowned out by the noise of the dam. Pushed away from each other by the currents, we were essentially alone with our thoughts, in a seemingly hopeless struggle against the force of nature.

Fighting to stay afloat, I was suddenly pulled deep under water, too deep to have any chance of pulling myself back up. So deep, I knew I had breathed my last breath. In a final state of disbelief, shocked that my life had ended so needlessly and quickly, I closed my eyes and relaxed.

The next thing I knew, I realized I was breathing again. I opened my eyes and saw the sky. I turned my head and saw that I was being pulled downstream away from the dam. "I'm alive, I'm alive!"

I screamed, as if convincing myself. Pulling my wits together, I watched out for onrushing boulders and swam ashore.

The force of the hydraulic had sucked me upstream where I had met the water rushing over the dam, which then drove me so far underwater that I escaped the grip of the hydraulic.

Lying on a rock near the shoreline, I looked upstream for George but he was gone. But only for a second. Pop! His helmeted head shot up from under the surface, and he started floating downstream. Upon seeing me, I heard him scream: "You're alive! You're alive!" I pulled him out of the water, amazed that we had both survived our reckless adventure.

Talking through the experience during our drive back home we both agreed that we had never experienced such powerful emotions. While I was drowning, I thought about how sad my parents would be when they learned that I had died and about my girlfriend, Paula (who's now my wife), and how she had told me to be careful when I left her earlier that morning. But I mainly thought about myself, about how sad it was that I was missing out on the last fifty years of my life.

By contrast, while struggling in the water, George told me he almost exclusively focused his thoughts on his one-year-old boy, Max, grieving over the thought that he wouldn't be there while Max grew up. At the time, I thought that our drowning had created equally powerful emotions in the two of us, even though we had thought about such different things. But in retrospect, now that I have kids—and now that I have had my ALS nightmare—I believe that George's emotions were ten times more powerful than my own.

Why am I telling you this story? It is practically gospel among most social scientists that social support is a key resource people draw upon in times of adversity. That it helps to have friends who can build driveways or provide a shoulder to cry on. But Scott's near-death experience—his narrow avoidance of a complete loss of communication—and George's near-drowning illustrate that receiving help doesn't give people a reason to live. In both of their cases, they felt it was vitally important to be engaged in other people's lives.

Always a Parent

Indeed, it is important to be actively engaged in people's lives. Scott, after all, said he wouldn't want to be kept alive on a ventilator if he couldn't communicate. Clearly, watching his kids grow up wasn't enough. He needed to be involved in their lives.

Six months into his bout with ALS, I asked Scott whether he would ever go on a ventilator, and he replied, rhetorically, "Wouldn't you want to see your boys grow up?" Spending a night in the Mackler home once after having moved to Ann Arbor, I realized that Scott was not simply watching his sons grow up. He was busy parenting them. We had finished dinner, and Scott was trying to talk to me with his Borg-like contraption but the computer was glitching out. Five minutes would go by between comprehensible sentences. Meanwhile, typical teenagers-in-the-house mayhem surrounded us. Noah was learning how to drive and was planning to take the car out with Alexander. Lynn tried to get Noah to allow his older brother to back the car out of their crowded driveway but this threatened Noah's teenage ego, so they battled over her request for a few hectic minutes. That conversation ended, and Lynn and I began talking about something else. Then Scott beeped at us with his computer to get our attention. He had managed to type out the words: "He can't drive." "Well he's just learning, honey," Lynn replied. "Give him a break." "No," Scott typed out with his eyeball. "Apologize or no driving." While arguing about the car situation, Noah had been rude to his mom. Lynn had ignored Noah's behavior, but Scott had not. He made sure that Noah apologized to his mom before he left the house or, in effect, he would be grounded. Disability or no disability, Scott remained the primary enforcer in the Mackler household.

On another visit to Scott's house, I went with Scott and Lynn to watch one of Noah's soccer games. Noah's team had surprised everyone but the Mackler family by dominating its conference due in no small part to Noah's accomplishments as goalie and midfielder (although not at the same time). Scott watched the game from the sideline, clicking and eyebrowing out occasional requests for me to get out of his field of vision or answering questions the rest of us had about the game we were watching. He managed to tell us what player ought to get credit for a goal when a crossing pass bounced off a defender's head into the goal. It was great fun watching the game with Scott, and I could see why he was eager to stick around and watch his boys grow up. But I was once again reminded of the nonpassivity of Scott's parental role when I returned home from Michigan and recevied an e-mail from Scott, including me on a message he had sent to Noah, giving him tips about how to improve his goal tending.

Scott's relationship with his two boys gave him a powerful reason to live. In this context, it is useful to remind ourselves of the distinction between moment-to-moment, mood-based happiness and meaningful or purpose-based happiness. Having adolescent kids often causes people to experience a greater than normal amount of negative moods. But it also fills people with a powerful sense of meaning and purpose, as they struggle to help their adolescents transition into early adulthood.

Too often, when researchers study the effects of social relationships on health and happiness, they focus solely on what people gain from social relationships. People with chronic illness receive physical and financial support from friends and family. But is it such support that brings people happiness? If Scott lost the ability to communicate, to take an extreme but very realistic example, he could continue to live as the passive recipient of love and support. But he would not choose to live under such circumstances. What gets Scott up and out of bed in the morning is not the physical therapy students who come to his house and lift up his flaccid body; it is the thought that the world needs him to figure out how to cure cocaine addiction, that his wife needs him to give her love and comfort when she is down, and that his boys need him the way they have always needed him—to be their loving but firm father.

So, Is It Better to Give Help or Receive It?

Numerous studies have shown that people with chronic illness who receive lots of social support live longer than those who do not. But these studies are now being challenged by my colleague Stephanie Brown, an evolutionary psychologist. Hypothesizing that there are evolutionary pressures for humans, as a species, to help each other out, she measured the mortality rate of a group of elderly people. As with previous studies, she found that people who receive substantial social support live longer than those who do not. However, this mortality benefit held up only if she ignored how much social support these people gave to others. When she statistically accounted both for social support given and received, she discovered that it was the *giving* of such support that predicted how long people would live. People who helped other people lived longer!

What could explain Brown's results? Helping others gives meaning and purpose to people's lives, and even improves people's moods. People may be hardwired to feel good about helping others. In fact, evolutionary psychologists are increasingly convinced that many of our moral attitudes evolved—that altruism and selflessness, despite seeming to contradict the survival of the fittest strain of evolutionary thinking, actually make people more fit to survive. Humans are so interconnected with each other that they depend on each other to survive. Thus, evolution has rewarded people who cooperate with others by making such actions pleasurable, thereby reducing the levels of their stress hormones, and so on, and so on.

If Brown is right, then being able to contribute to others may be one of the most important things people experiencing adversity can do to overcome their circumstances. People need to find ways to contribute to others.

Without his VisionKey program and without any chance to rid the world of cocaine addiction or to help his sons navigate their late teen years, Scott Mackler would be dead. At least in Scott's case, then, Brown's theory is right on target. Being able to help others really can have survival benefits.

The Struggle to Overcome Small Nuisances

I fear I have made it sound all too easy, as if, in the face of debilitating illness, people simply mobilize their emotional resources, minimize their pain, and, with a touch of DNA and a little help from their friends, find themselves almost as happy as they were before they became sick. I have described that when Greg Hughes woke up from his coma he was so glad to be alive that he barely took notice of his missing legs and that Scott Mackler, after suffering immensely in the first few months of his illness, reclaimed his optimistic outlook on life once it became clear that he had amyotrophic lateral sclerosis (ALS).

But such rapid and complete adaptation is far from universal. For people with serious illness or disability, the search for happiness is often a struggle. Although 90 percent of people say they are very satisfied or somewhat satisfied with their lives, only 74 percent of people with a single disability say so, and the number drops to 57 percent for those with more than one disability and to 49 percent for those with severe disabilities. Severe disability is not as devastating as most people expect—with a fifty-fifty chance of happiness being much higher than most people predict. But neither is it as inconsequential as Greg's and Scott's experiences might suggest.

In fact, Greg and Scott continued to face new challenges arising from their respective disabilities. Scott's illness continued to progress; with each stage of his illness, he had to overcome new obstacles. Unlike Scott, Greg faced a "stable" disability. But he still had not found out what it was like to re-enter the real world, outside the comfortable confines of the rehabilitation hospital. Greg would face many new challenges upon returning home, challenges that would threaten his emotional stability.

Greg and Scott would both learn that even though they had already suffered dramatic losses, it would be the seemingly tiny nuisances that would stand as the greatest threat to their emotional resilience.

Pain, Boredom, and Household Chores

I first visited Greg at his house a month after he returned home from the rehabilitation hospital, on the day his brother and friends built him the new driveway. I walked up the ramp to his front door—a ramp built by those same friends—and Greg's wife, Ruth, greeted me at the door. She brought me back to the dining room where Greg was sitting at the table working on a plastic NASCAR model. Having just finished spray-painting pieces of the model, he was waiting for them to dry so he could assemble the car. We exchanged pleasantries and had a piece of bundt cake, while Greg and Ruth told the story about getting stuck in the driveway. They were both quite animated in accounting the details of that rainy night, laughing about what a messy spectacle they had been when they arrived at the party. I marveled at how well Greg was adjusting to life at home.

But Greg would not let me hold on to this illusion, explaining that things were not going as well as he had hoped. He pointed to a shelf full of NASCAR models he had put together over the past month and, next to them, a series of wood burnings he had also completed. On their own, each of the finished works looked like an enjoyable way to spend some time. But crammed together on the shelf, this gallery of objects looked like the work of someone with an extremely large amount of time on his hands.

Before Greg lost his legs, he worked seventy hours a week at the service station and spent a fair portion of his remaining time fixing stuff around the house or participating in outdoor hobbies. Now he was unemployed and most of the work he used to do around the house was either too low to the ground for him to perform (it being difficult to stoop over from his wheelchair) or too close to the ceiling for him to reach. Because it was January and his wheelchair was not designed to slog through the Michigan snow, he couldn't spend much time outside. Even the sidewalks in town were too rough and tumble for Greg to traverse in his wheelchair, and he felt the streets were unsafe. Cooped up inside his house, without a job and without the ability to pursue most of his hobbies, Greg had a hundred hours of extra time to kill each week.

For many people with new disabilities, their days in the rehabilitation hospital are the most depressing ones of their lives, a time when they must confront their new disabilities even as their emotional and physical reserves have been utterly depleted by injury or illness. The strange hospital environment only makes matters worse for many patients, exposed as they are to bad food and unfamiliar roommates. Recognizing how difficult this time can be, rehabilitation teams routinely include clinical psychologists who meet with patients to help them through these often dark days.

Greg Hughes felt almost no need for such help. He maintained an amazingly positive attitude throughout his hospital stay and was confident that his emotional outlook would continue to improve. Each day he stayed in the hospital, he got stronger, became more adept at maneuvering from place to place, and felt less pain at his amputation sites. Things would only continue to get better at home, he thought, where he would be able to sleep in his own bed, eat his own food, and wear his own clothes.

Suffering from High Expectations

From that rain-soaked night in his driveway, Greg soon learned that coming home creates a whole new set of challenges. The hospital was full of activity, with physical therapy and occupational therapy sessions, bedside examinations by his doctors and nurses, and visits with friends and family. The hospital was a place of rapid progress. At first Greg was so weak from being in a coma that he could barely scratch his nose. And from this starting point, he could notice daily improvement in his arm strength. By contrast, home days were filled with much less activity and social contact. Greg had not anticipated how bored he would get with so many fewer distractions or how much less human contact he would have with most of his time spent at home with no one other than Ruth. He had not imagined the frustration he would feel sitting at home staring at some home fix-it job that he could not attend to, like seeing a window that was not quite tracking the way it should and not being able to fix it! He had not realized how much slower he would improve once at home, with his strength growing, perhaps, by the month and not by the day. And the time was soon approaching when he would no longer get any stronger.

Greg was suffering from his high expectations. When staying in the hospital, he'd imagined all the benefits of home life without considering its drawbacks. He also fast-forwarded his recovery, imagining what it would feel like to be as strong as he expected to be, with well-healed stump wounds and maybe even with a new job in a machine shop. But when he got home, he realized that these improvements were going to come much more slowly than he had imagined and that other parts of his life at home would not be as idyllic as he had predicted.

Greg was frustrated because his toolshed was staring at him through the window from fifteen feet away, and he could not cross the snowy yard to look inside. Greg's frustrations reminded me of two friends of mine who, after moving out of New York City, complained about the paucity of cultural events in their new town. When I reminded them that they were too busy with kids and work to be able to attend many cultural events anyway, they said that simply *knowing* there are lots of cultural events around them is more important than actually being able to attend any events. A similar frustration seemed to be affecting Greg. The task of winterizing his home had hardly been a major highlight of his pre-amputation life. But take away his ability to winterize his own home, and . . . aaaaargh!

Greg tried to alleviate his boredom by keeping busy, reading, watching movies, and doing other activities that would be unaffected by his disability. But even these activities were shut off to him; distracted and tormented by the pain, he couldn't concentrate on them.

The most severe pains were what doctors call phantom pains, pains that occur in nonexistent limbs. "It feels like someone is grabbing on to my legs above the knee [one of the knees that no longer exists] and yanking on the tendons as they run down to my foot." As he described this to me, he squeezed one hand into a fist, as if it was grabbing on to a bunch of strings, and placed his other hand on to his hip, pretending to pull at the strings with all his might. Watching him pantomime this sensation practically sent pain shooting down *my* leg tendons. Seeing me grimace, Greg could not resist embellishing his description. "Sometimes it's like the bones in my stumps are exposed, and someone is jabbing a big metal rod into it with a sledgehammer. When the hammer hits, I am literally knocked back on my chair, with parts from whatever model I'm working on flying in the air. I'll scream so loud it scares my dogs."

Less severe and yet more troubling than his phantom pains were the paresthesias he was experiencing, continuous tingly sensations at his stumps where his nerve endings had been damaged. These paresthesias made Greg feel like he was sitting on a pile of tiny pins and needles. The pain was not intense when compared to his phantom pains. On a 0-to-10 scale, for example, his phantom pains registered something above 12, but these phantom pains never lasted long. The paresthesias, however, lingered in the background, a mere 3 or 4 out of 10, but persistent and irritating enough that they made it difficult for him to concentrate during the day and almost impossible for him to sleep at night.

Because of advances in pharmacology and anesthesiology, physicians like to tell patients that they can relieve them of any pains they experience, whether from metastatic cancer, osteoarthritis, or limb amputations. And this is true. With enough morphine, physicians can render anyone unconscious or at least put them into a drunken stupor, thereby making them oblivious to their pain. But most people do not want pain relief to come at the price of their consciousness. They want to be alert enough to read a book, without fear that the book might fly across the room at any moment when the tendon-puller shows up. Medicating people with severe pain is often a delicate balancing act, and Greg's doctors had not yet found the proper balance. He was taking a slew of pain medications, sleeping pills, and nerve-soothers, without significant pain relief— but with plenty of side effects. He felt so doped up by his medications that he had a hard time concentrating. "I'm frustrated," he told me, "but I'm going back in another week or so, and I'll see if the doctors have any new ideas about how to control my pain."

To get Greg's mind off his pain and frustration, I tried to change the topic and asked Ruth how her job was going. I soon found out another fact about his return to home life that Greg had not anticipated—that he would be living with an unemployed wife. "The economy slowed down," Ruth told me, "and my boss figured I was the best person to lay off, seeing how I had missed so much work lately anyway, visiting Greg at the hospital." Rather than improving the emotional atmosphere of the room, my shifting of the topic had simply augmented their collective sense of discouragement.

Greg also felt frustrated, and a bit guilty, about having to make Ruth take over so many tasks around the house, such as the winterizing and fix-it jobs. Hoping again to switch the conversation to a more positive topic, I asked Greg what chores he was doing around the house to make up for all of Ruth's new duties. Ruth leapt on my question first. "Not a damn thing! I try to get him to help with dishes or cooking, and he just sits around." Greg tried to defuse the situation with a joke. "I told her that I'm happy to vacuum as long as she pushes me back and forth on my wheelchair." Ruth was not amused, perhaps because she had heard that joke too many times already. Greg continued, "I just hate housework, I always have. That's why I liked fixing stuff around the house while Ruth cooked and cleaned. I can't bear the thought of helping do that housework."

Early in their relationship, many spouses squabble over dishes or lawn work, but eventually, most spouses specialize. One person can be counted on to mow the lawn and the other to empty the trash. In a healthy marriage, both partners end up reasonably convinced that the other partner is pulling his or her fair share of the load. Prior to Greg's amputations, he and Ruth had reached this type of equilibrium. But now, their equilibrium had been thrown off and they had yet to find a new one.

Greg was a happier man at the rehabilitation hospital than he was at home. In the rehabilitation hospital, he seemed to have adapted to his disability. But his transition to home life had proven that adaptation is an ongoing process. Greg was suffering because the reality of his home life did not match up to his expectations. In imagining life at home, he thought about all the things that would be better than his rehabilitation surroundings—the food, the comforts, the smells. He had not anticipated all the boredom and loneliness . . . and pain.

Sensitization: The Flip Side of Adaptation

Not all adversities are created equal. Some are much greater tests of people's emotional resilience. As I explained earlier, most adversities are better handled within the rich give and take of healthy social relationships. And uncertain fates are typically harder to cope with than certain ones. But Greg's response to his various pains belies some of this supposed wisdom. In theory, he ought to be able to adapt to the constant background of his paresthesias more easily than the intermittent shock of his phantom pains. And yet, without minimizing the unpleasantness of the phantom pains, Greg expressed special dismay over his paresthesias.

Greg's intolerance of these paresthesias demonstrates that adaptation is not the universal human response to adversity. Sometimes, instead of getting used to annoyances or unpleasantries, people get increasingly bothered by them over time. When Greg first began experiencing paresthesias, he found them mildly annoying. But when they persisted, he had an increasingly difficult time ignoring them.

I had a roommate in college who made an obnoxious sucking sound when he chewed his food. I didn't even notice this sound at first, but once I noticed it, it began to bother me and, over time, it drove me crazy. The slightest slurp and I was beside myself with anxiety. Have you ever been bothered by a dripping sound from a leaky faucet? Such a sound can wiggle its way into your brain until it is impossible to ignore. Rather than adapting to what at most should be a minor annoyance, you actually become *sensitized* to it.

Sensitization is the flip side of adaptation. When people adapt to a circumstance, their emotional response to it diminishes over time. When people become sensitized, their emotional response increases. Social scientists have little idea why some people adapt to circumstances and others become sensitized to them, nor why some circumstances are more likely to lead to sensitization than others. And they have barely begun to explore situations where early adaptation collapses to sensitization—situations where people summon the emotional strength to deal with a bad circumstance for a while but soon drain their emotional reserves so that a problem they previously ignored becomes intolerable.

Minor Annoyances Take on a Life of Their Own

It is clear that some miseries *do* become more miserable over time. Noise is one such misery. Most college students, for example, say they aren't bothered by dormitory noise in the first few weeks of the semester but are highly annoyed by it later in the semester. Talk to people several months after a busy highway opens in their neighborhood and most expect that they will get used to it. But one year later, such expectations are gone, and people are much more likely to spontaneously complain of the noise. Pain, too, is something people often have difficulty adapting to. My research team has found that the strongest predictor of happiness and quality of life after an amputation is neither the cause of the amputation (whether it resulted from sudden trauma or chronic infection) nor the level of amputation (whether it is above or below the knee, for example), but whether the amputation is complicated by chronic pain.

I expect that things like noise and pain lead to sensitization because of the pervasive way they interfere with people's activities.

People's well-being is greatly enhanced if they can pursue what University of Chicago psychologist Mihaly Csikszentmihalyi calls "flow" activities—the kinds of activities where time flies and people lose awareness of anything outside the activity. A piano piece, a tennis match, a novel—whatever the activity—people thrive when they pursue things they can be fully engaged in.

Greg Hughes couldn't concentrate well enough to follow the thread of a novel. He couldn't even lose himself in an action flick, plagued as he was by the constant distraction of his paresthesias and the intermittent horrors of his phantom pains. He was learning that minor annoyances can become maddeningly irritating when they persist. He was gaining firsthand insight into the effectiveness of Chinese water tortures.

My Kingdom for a Cough!

Eighteen months into his illness, Scott Mackler was experiencing a Chinese water torture of his own as progressive muscle weakness made it increasingly difficult to clear his salivary secretions. The lung doctor had recently measured Scott's breathing muscles and found they had less than 5 percent of their normal strength, a weakness more profound than he had ever seen in someone who was not on a ventilator. Years of fanatical exercise had strengthened Scott's heart and lungs—and had also increased the efficiency of oxygen exchange throughout his body—putting off the day when he'd need a breathing machine.

Yet, despite being strong enough to breathe on his own, Scott was beginning to suffer because of his respiratory weakness. He could summon the strength to take routine breaths, but he could not muster the force to cough, making it difficult for him to clear respiratory secretions from his airways. To compound his problems,

Scott's throat muscles were so weak that he often had a hard time swallowing his saliva. Consequently, his saliva would trickle down the back of his throat into his trachea, adding to the volume of respiratory secretions collecting in his lungs. Scott was drowning in his own spit.

Most people think of coughing as a bad thing. We cough when we are sick; coughs give us sore throats, strain our rib muscles, and inevitably interfere with slow movements of Beethoven's symphonies. But at this point in time, Scott would have paid handsomely for the ability to produce a deep, full-chested cough. For most people, when a little liquid goes down their windpipe, a vigorous cough sends the fluid on its way. But Scott's breathing muscles were too weak for him to cough effectively, so when he inhaled his saliva it had nowhere to go but down into his lungs. Meanwhile, the nerve receptors in his trachea sensed the fluid and responded accordingly, signaling to the cough center in Scott's brain that it was time to act. So, Scott would try to cough, but too ineffectively to clear the airway. As a result, he was inundated with a constant urge to cough. A cough, a cough—my kingdom for a good, hearty cough!

A Good, Deep Sigh

How about sighing? Most people think of sighing as a sign of boredom or a gesture of relief. But many experts believe it is a necessary bodily function, opening up airways deep in the base of people's lungs, and thereby reducing the chance that the airways will become infected. To grasp how this could be, it helps to think of the lungs as a pair of Slinkies. If you grab one end of a Slinky and hold it up in the air, the part in your hand will be stretched out by the weight of the Slinky, but the lower part will remain relatively compact— the adjacent coils will still touch each other. The lungs hang from the top of people's rib cages, like the imaginary Slinky in your hand, and are pulled downward by gravity. Thus, like the Slinky, the airspaces at the top of people's lungs are stretched out, while those at the bottom remain relatively compact, with the airways slightly collapsed, even touching each other. Fluid and debris that make their way down into this portion of people's lungs stick to these adjacent surfaces and fester. A good sigh, like a hand stretching a Slinky to its limits, pulls the adjacent tissues apart from each other, allowing the lung spaces the breathing space, so to speak, to rid themselves of debris, thereby reducing the chance of infection.

Because he lacked the strength for a big cough or a deep sigh, Scott's airways were becoming congested. Saliva was accumulating in his airways, creating a frequent and irritating need for half-coughs, or quarter-coughs, or whatever Scott could muster. Similar to the paresthesias Greg Hughes was experiencing, Scott's constant urge to cough was maddening. More worrisome, however, was the fear that he would choke. So, he decided that it was time for a tracheotomy: A surgeon would cut a hole in his trachea, right below his Adam's apple, and he'd be able to breathe through his neck, meaning that saliva collecting in his mouth would no longer threaten his life. Just as important, Scott would be able to use a ventilator to breathe at night. He was making it through the night on his own lung power right now but soon he would be too weak. A ventilator might help him rest better.

A tracheotomy is usually a simple surgical procedure. But within thirty-six hours of his surgery, Scott spiked a fever and his white blood cell count shot up, signs that he had contracted an infection. His doctors soon discovered that he had contracted pseudomonas pneumonia, a dangerous bacterial infection that, in his case, was resistant to most available antibiotics. Scott might have caught the infection because his lungs lately had been seeped in so much extra fluid. More likely, a surgeon or a nurse or a respiratory technologist had inadvertently touched Scott's tracheotomy site with hands or gloves that had recently bumped into some pseudomonas bacteria.

Whatever the cause of Scott's infection, he was in big trouble. Pseudomonas is a deadly bug, even for people with normal muscle strength. In his weakened state, Scott realized he might not survive. Lynn told me later, however, that she could tell Scott was not ready to die. The light in his eyes never dimmed as he determinedly fought off the infection, with the help, of course, of the most powerful antibiotics his doctors could get their hands on. For a week, Scott's condition was critical. Then, his fevers subsided and his oxygen levels returned to normal. He was clearing the infection.

Only then did I learn, out in Michigan, that my friend had almost died. I quickly made plans to visit him. I arrived in Philadelphia a month or so after he came home from the hospital. As with previous visits, I walked down the hallway toward Scott's office with mixed feelings, excited to see him, while dreading the thought of seeing how far his disease had progressed since my last visit. Before this visit, my dread was usually alleviated by Scott's sense of humor. As awful as it was to see Scott in a wheelchair barely able to move his pinky finger, the sarcastic messages he would relay to me through his computer would reassure me that Scott was still Scott and, more important, would keep me so busy trying to think of good retorts that I had little time to feel sorry for him.

On this visit, however, my dread was not so quickly alleviated. Scott was still quite weak from his pneumonia. *Weak* probably sounds like a strange word to apply to someone who, on a good day, can barely lift his pinky finger. But Scott was more fatigued than I had ever seen before, and the fatigue showed in his mood. Scott's life is full of frustrations that would drive most people crazy—the slowness of communicating through his computer and the itches he cannot scratch because of his muscle weakness. Scott had previously amazed me with his ability to deal with these irritations; he recognized that they were an unavoidable part of his life and managed to focus on other, more important things. But now Scott was increasingly bothered by these nuisances. If his nurse, Dana, could not scratch his itch right away, he became distressed; if his computer crashed, he acted almost like the rest of us would, with a desire to smash his laptop against the wall.

To compound his difficulties, Scott was struggling to adjust to life with his tracheotomy. The tracheotomy had improved Scott's life in many of the ways he had hoped it would. He was sleeping better at night because the work of breathing had been taken over by the ventilator. Lynn was sleeping better, too, knowing that if Scott stopped breathing in the middle of the night, the ventilator would alert her to the problem. And Scott no longer worried that he would choke to death on his own saliva. Now with the tracheotomy, Lynn or a nurse could suction Scott whenever his trachea or upper airways filled up with fluid. Scott no longer needed to cough to get these fluids out.

Oh, but the suctioning! The first time I saw Scott receive suctioning, I felt a new level of sadness for my friend. Dana pulled out a plastic tube, attached one end to the suctioning machine, and then snaked the other end down Scott's trachea, through the hole below his Adam's apple. She flipped a switch and the machine purred to life, vacuuming out the inside of Scott's trachea. As soon as the suctioning began, Scott's body arched back violently. I was surprised at the power remaining in Scott's back muscles and doubted he could have summoned that kind of muscle activity without experiencing a great deal of pain. As Dana suctioned his airway, Scott gave me a helpless look as if I could somehow intervene to end his suffering. But, of course, I could not. Scott would suffer every thirty minutes or so for the rest of the time I visited him that day.

Continuing to Adapt to Adversity

As I wrote earlier, Scott coped with his rapidly progressing illness in part by imagining what his life would be like as he got weaker.

He imagined losing strength in his legs long before he did so, and these imaginings helped him prepare for the eventual loss of his legs. In effect, Scott coped with each progression of his illness by pre-adapting to it.

But Scott had never given much thought to respiratory secretions until he reached the point where they were torturing him. He had never contemplated what it would feel like to live with a constant urge to cough. So now, he had to adapt to a challenge that he had not prepared to face.

Unfortunately, tragically even, Scott's tracheotomy had not eliminated his constant desire to cough. Patients typically experience transient increases in their respiratory secretions after a tracheotomy. But never content with being typical, Scott's body persisted in being an overachieving secretory machine and Scott was losing patience. He would request a back-arching suctioning session, which would pull a little fluid from his tracheotomy. Ten minutes later, he would ask to be suctioned again. He had reached the point, it appeared, where three or four stray drops of saliva in his airways were enough to make him uncomfortable.

By midafternoon, Scott was ready to leave work and go home, having become exhausted trying to squeeze in tiny bits of laboratory work in between his suctioning sessions. So Dana and I (mainly Dana!) loaded Scott into his van and drove back to his house in Delaware. When we arrived home, I realized why Scott was so eager to leave the lab. His oldest son, Alexander, was returning home from his first semester in college. Alexander had not gone very far away to attend college. In fact, he had enrolled at the University of Pennsylvania where he visited his father at his laboratory almost every day. Yet as often as Scott saw Alexander, he was still excited to have him back at home.

Alexander is a gregarious young man with a knack for banter reminiscent of his father. He was in a hilarious mood that night, amusing us all with stories of freshman debauchery. Rifting through the mail, he found a package from the summer camp he had worked at, containing a CD-ROM video highlighting that summer's activities. He quickly popped the CD into Scott's computer and entertained us with stories of the various kids pictured in the video.

Distracted by all the entertainment, Scott was able to forgo suctioning for a while. But Dana's workday was ending, so she suctioned him one more time for good measure and headed home while Alexander and I assured her that Scott was in capable hands.

Our assurances were premature. Usually, Lynn would have arrived home by the time Dana left, but she was stuck at work that night. Normally, another helper would have also been on hand—Jill, a physical therapy graduate student who now lived in the basement. But Jill was out of town on vacation, leaving only three pairs of "capable" hands to take care of Scott—me, Alexander, and Noah, Alexander's sixteen-year-old brother, who had just arrived home from high school. Noah had spent a lot of time at home with his dad over the past month and was tuned in to his dad's suctioning needs in ways that Alexander and I were not. But Noah was upstairs in his room, so Scott was essentially in the hands of two people who had never suctioned him. Alexander and I were in the kitchen with Scott watching the computer CD when Scott began feeling secretions in his airway. He asked us to call Noah downstairs to suction him. Alexander yelled upstairs and Noah bellowed back that he'd be down in a minute. A few minutes passed with no sign of Noah. Scott was breathing fine but was uncomfortable and not at all happy that immediate suctioning was unavailable. Alexander yelled upstairs two more times. Finally, Noah wound his way downstairs, muttering under his breath about needing to be able to go to the bathroom once in a while. He dutifully suctioned his dad and headed back upstairs.

Normally, Alexander and I would be pretty entertaining company. (Normally, Alexander and *anybody* would be pretty entertaining company.) But obsessed as he was with his secretions, Scott was not appreciating our company. After spending the day at work with Dana, who suctioned him on demand, it was hard for him to tolerate the long intervals between suctioning.

The Nuisance of Sensation

I doubt I need to convince anyone how terrible ALS can be. I had watched ALS strip my friend of almost every bodily function. I had seen it strip him of the strength to run a marathon or scramble across a tennis court to where he now couldn't lift his hands off the armrests of his wheelchair.

But ALS is very specific in its destructions. It hadn't robbed Scott of bowel or bladder function, a small consolation, perhaps, but a welcome one. Even more important, it hadn't stolen strength from his eye muscles, meaning he could still see normally and could communicate through VisionKey. And, most important, it hadn't made a dent in Scott's big beautiful brain, failing to alter his intellect, sense of humor, or outlook on life.

ALS had also failed to impair any of Scott's senses. He could taste, smell, hear, see, and feel as well as ever. However, in sparing his feelings—his sensory feelings, that is—it had thrown another set of nuisances in his path. Scott also had become obsessed with the position of his elbows and hands. He was almost completely paralyzed now, so if his elbow was resting in an uncomfortable position, he could no longer make the tiny adjustments that used to bring him relief. He was obsessed with his pants legs, too. A wrinkle under his knees would bore into his sensory cortex until someone could smooth it out and relieve his discomfort. He was obsessed also with his inability to fidget—he couldn't shift his weight or reposition his limbs and was discovering that all his fidgeting over the previous years was not merely a sign of his hyperactivity, but was also an important bodily function.

To begin to appreciate Scott's situation, try sitting in a chair for an hour without moving a muscle. You will find that a comfortable position never remains comfortable for long. Most of us continually reposition our bodies, even in our sleep, to keep from putting pressure on one given spot for too long. Scott cannot reposition himself; his body senses this, sending signals to his brain every few minutes telling him it is time to move his elbow, or his leg, or his buttocks.

One of the cruelest aspects of ALS is that it spares sensory nerves. People with quadriplegia can sit in wheelchairs and be comfortable for long periods of time, never bothered when one of their arms lies in an awkward position. Scott, on the other hand, with his senses at full strength, will feel a small wrinkle in his sleeve; his arm, completely dead weight now, will lie upon the wrinkle and slowly get uncomfortable. After a while, he will ask someone to shift his arm to another position or to smooth out his shirt. Then, over the next few minutes, he will learn whether the repositioning has simply placed another part of his limb on yet another wrinkle. That night at his house, waiting for Lynn to return, it felt like the three of us were constantly either suctioning Scott or repositioning his limbs. His bodily irritations had become all-consuming.

As a physician, I had always thought that ALS was doing patients a favor by preserving their sensory nerves. People with spinal cord injuries who have lost sensation often develop horrible pressure sores. Sitting in a bed or a wheelchair for hours on end without moving interrupts blood flow to the weight-bearing parts of people's bodies. If someone with a spinal cord injury is allowed to sit for long periods in one position, he will not feel a pressure sore developing. Actor Christopher Reeve, in fact, died from an infection that spread from a pressure sore. From my medical standpoint, then, spinal cord injuries seemed much worse than ALS because they led to so many pressure sores and infections and other complications that patients might not be aware of. But now, visiting Scott, I realized the daily grind of living with ALS and all those damn sensory nerves. With semi-hourly repositioning, a person with a spinal cord injury can usually avoid pressure sores. On the other hand, Scott was a prisoner of his sensory nerves, completely dependent on other people for every itch and scratch and wrinkle that traveled up to his sensory cortex.

At the time Scott was suffering so much from his secretions, he was less than one month removed from his life and death struggle with pneumonia. I could tell he lacked some of the emotional strength to cope with his illness. I was very worried that he was beginning a downward spiral that would lead to his death. So I traveled back again to the Philadelphia area a month later and spent another night at Scott's house.

I was delighted to discover that Scott was stronger than he had been on my previous visit. His muscles were not stronger, of course, but he was more alert, more stubborn, and more combative—more Scott-like. He still needed to have his arms and legs repositioned frequently, but less frequently than a month earlier, and his requests for such intervention were less desperate and impatient.

At wit's end over the outpouring of fluid building up in his trachea, he had begun requesting regular infusions of lidocaine into his windpipe. A close cousin of novocaine, lidocaine is a local anesthetic. When infused into his trachea, it would temporarily reduce Scott's desire to cough. Too much lidocaine and Scott would not sense any need to cough or to be suctioned and would be at risk for lung infections. But when used appropriately, it stopped Scott's coughing cycles without putting his lungs at terrible risk.

The question remained, however, as to what constituted appropriate use. On the night of my second posttracheotomy visit, Lynn and Jill were both at home, and Alexander had returned to college. With so much competent help available, Scott was almost always in the presence of someone who could quickly interpret and fulfill his needs. But it still wasn't going to be an easy night for Scott. Lynn was concerned about how often he was requesting lidocaine infusions. Scott was producing fewer secretions than he had a month earlier but still could not tolerate any amount of fluid in his trachea. He would ask to be suctioned, and Lynn or Jill would comply. Five minutes later he would ask to be suctioned again, or he'd ask for suctioning with a lidocaine "chaser." Finally, after requesting some combination of suctioning and lidocaine three times in less than half an hour, Lynn refused to comply. "Scott, I have sucked you dry, honey. You've got to learn to deal with it!" Later that night, frustrated by his frequent suctioning requests, Lynn chewed Scott out for complaining too much.

Now, Lynn is an amazing person. She is a world-class researcher with millions of dollars of National Institutes of Health (NIH) funding and a top-notch clinician who takes care of professional and Olympic athletes. She loves Scott unconditionally, but she is hardly a "yes" woman and perfectly comfortable with chewing him out for feeling sorry for himself. Lynn's actions could be viewed as harsh, picking on a poor guy who does not have the strength to turn his head. But Lynn was expecting to live with Scott for a long time, and so she needed to find a way for both of them to adapt to his illness. Lynn knew she couldn't attend to Scott's needs every five minutes for the next twenty years. Even more important, she recognized that if Scott required assistance every five minutes, he would never get any work done and would never have any time to communicate meaningful thoughts to his friends and his family.

Lynn was pushing Scott to adapt to his situation, knowing that if he could get used to these discomforts—put them out of his mind for five minutes—his life would be better. If he could find a way to numb himself to these little irritations, rather than become sensitized to them, he would be much happier. Scott was learning that adapting to ALS was an ongoing process and that those aspects of his illness that he used to fear the most—the paralysis and the inability to talk—were now much less bothersome than all the little inconveniences and nuisances beginning to accumulate. But Scott is as stubborn and strong-willed as any person I've met. And he was not giving in to those sufferings. Even on that frustrating and emotionally charged night, Scott was showing renewed signs of the strength and positive attitude that had served him so well over the past year and a half.

An hour or so after being told off by Lynn, he asked her to suction him again and she told him to wait a bit longer. A few minutes later, Lynn left the room and Scott beckoned for Jill to give him a lidocaine infusion. She gave him a reluctant look, well aware that Lynn was trying to reduce Scott's need for lidocaine. But Scott returned her gaze with sad, puppy-dog eyes and a mischievous half-grin; Jill had no choice but to sneak a little lidocaine into Scott's trachea behind Lynn's back.

Indeed, at that moment, the anesthetic benefits of that lidocaine infusion were paltry compared to the joy of pulling a fast one on Lynn.

Money Matters

Greg Hughes has never been a wealthy man. Then again, he has not been a man of expensive tastes or habits either. He and his wife, Ruth, have always been quite comfortable in their two-bedroom, single-story house, surrounded by pets and motor vehicles. Their combined incomes placed them solidly in the middle class, which left them with more than enough money to pursue their favorite hobbies. With no children, they didn't fret about future college tuition payments, and with the cost of living so low in Dansville, Michigan, they never felt as if they were living paycheck to paycheck.

When Greg lost his legs their financial situation changed dramatically. Gone was Greg's income and so too was Ruth's for a while when she was laid off from her job. To make matters worse, Greg had never invested in disability insurance, so they had to live off their life savings for six months until social security kicked in. Poring over the numbers, they were confident they could come up with enough money for the next few mortgage payments but after that things looked pretty iffy.

Then came the night of the rainstorm, when Greg and Ruth showed up to that party drenched and muddy from their driveway ordeal. The party they attended that night was not just any party. It was a welcome home party for Greg, and the main thrust of the evening was to raise money to help him and Ruth in their time of need. No elaborate gifts. No plaques or mementos. Just plain cold cash.

Greg and Ruth described the party to me as if they were still trying to convince themselves it had happened. "We came into the banquet hall expecting to see a couple dozen close friends," Greg told me. "But the place was standing room only." Perhaps worried that thoughts about the turnout would give Greg a big head, Ruth quickly cut him off, quipping that most people had shown up that night not because they thought highly of Greg but because they were looking for an excuse to party. But Ruth was only kidding, and the actions of all these partygoers made it clear that most of them crammed into the banquet hall that night because they were touched by Greg's situation and wanted to help. "My friends came up with all kinds of different ways to get people to part with their money," Greg explained. "They had a fifty-fifty lottery, where half the winnings were supposed to go to me and the other half to the person with the winning ticket, except the gal who had the winning ticket turned her half of the winnings over to me." He continued describing how generous everyone was. "The waitress working at the banquet hall . . . gave me all her tips, too. Local businesses chipped in and donated goods for an auction. I mean, I have never seen anything like it!" By the end of the night, probably after everyone had had a few beers, people were sneaking up behind Greg and slipping cash into the back of his wheelchair.

Greg and Ruth went home that night with $7,000, and the assurance they would be able to make a few extra mortgage payments.

Cash Is Cool

As Greg and Ruth's story illustrates, money matters: no money, no mortgage payment; no cash, no car; no funds, no food. It is obvious that money is a crucial means to very important ends. In fact, as author and psychologist Mihaly Csikszentmihalyi discovered when doing research on his book *Flow*, when people are asked what single change in their life would make them happier, their most common answer is "more money." Money is one of the most important driving forces behind many people's lives. People put up with mediocre jobs because of golden handcuffs. Hundreds of thousands of people play state lotteries because they think a big win will improve their lives.

And this belief—that money will bring happiness—has become much more prevalent over the past several decades. According to psychologist David Myers, in 1965, more than 80 percent of U.S. college students said they were going to college to develop a meaningful philosophy of life. By 2000, almost three-quarters said they came to college to increase their earning power.

Nevertheless, over the past decade, leading experts have written scientific articles, penned popular books, and spoken on television to tell people that money is not nearly as important as they think it is. Remember psychologist Philip Brickman's lottery winner study from Chapter 1? Despite winning gobs of money, Brickman's lottery winners were *barely* happier than other people. Some might counter that winning the lottery is not a very typical way of acquiring money, making it hard to generalize from the experience of lottery winners to that of other people with similar amounts of money. Lottery winners receive their good fortune in one fell swoop, usually with great fanfare, causing old high school "friends" and long-lost relatives to show up at their doorstep asking them for small business loans.

What about other wealthy people, then? Are they a lot happier than the rest of us mortals? Once again the answer is no. They are not much, if any, happier. The average happiness of someone making $220,000 per year is *barely* greater than someone making $50,000 per year, and that difference is only discernable by studying large numbers of people. In fact, when Ed Diener, perhaps the world's foremost expert on well-being, surveyed forty-nine of the richest people in America, he found that one-third of these fabulously wealthy people were *less happy* than an average person would be. Think about that. Many people spend the better part of their youths pursuing wealth. Would they do that if they knew that becoming a multi-gazillionaire would still leave them a one in three chance of being less happy than their middle-class friends?

Almost everywhere scientists look, they find that money doesn't matter much. That people are happy almost regardless of their incomes. They find that people in modestly wealthy countries such as Spain are as happy as people in wealthy countries like the United States. They find that within any given country, there is often very little relationship between money and happiness across time. For example, researchers have been measuring happiness and income in the United States for more than fifty years. Inflation-adjusted income nearly doubled in the United States between 1945 and 1970. It practically doubled again between 1970 and 2000. Yet, despite this quadrupling of American incomes, people's overall happiness has not changed one iota. Americans are no happier now than they reported being in 1945, 1965, or 1985.

When Money Does Matter

The only place researchers have found that money really seems to matter is at the very lowest rungs of the income ladder. At low incomes, the relationship between money and happiness is quite strong; people who are extremely poor are usually less happy than people who are only slightly poor. The importance of money in these contexts makes sense. For people with very little money, an extra $10,000 can be the difference between making the mortgage payment and being evicted. A little extra cash can be the difference between living paycheck to paycheck versus planning a more stable future.

Can Money Overcome Adversity?

What role does money play in people's ability to overcome adversity? As Greg and Ruth's situation illustrates, some adversities like severe disability can take away people's financial stability. Greg and Ruth never used to live paycheck to paycheck. Suddenly they were struggling to make it to their first disability check. But is their experience typical? Does money play a bigger role in people's emotional lives when they confront adversity? And why, against all common sense, does it seem to matter so little to everyone else?

Against Common Sense

I have always considered myself to be a man of simple pleasures. I have no interest in expensive cars, fancy wines, or fine clothes. I enjoy books but don't see the point in collecting first editions. I love tennis but don't belong to any club, seeing no point in spending money when the public courts near my house have only a handful of cracks on them. Obsessed with music, I enjoy countless hours playing piano at no financial cost other than tuning the instrument once a year.

And yet when I reflect on my hobbies, it is easy to see how money has made me happy. For example, when I lived in Chicago many years ago, my aging Honda Civic was broken into four times in one year. I drove the car for several more years without bothering to replace the stolen radio. When I finally bought a new Civic in 1994, I was ecstatic to be able to listen to music on my new car's radio. I quickly realized how stupid I had been for refusing to replace the old car's radio, forgoing hours of music listening because I was so cheap.

Two years later, my new car was stolen, borrowed actually, by my wife, who snuck it off to an electronics shop where she paid for them to install a CD player, since I had been too cheap to pay for one when I had bought the car. Once again, I quickly realized the stupidity of my ways. Thanks to the money Paula spent, I could now drive anywhere and listen to music that I loved!

Finally, this last Christmas my wife gave me an iPod, and I'm listening to classical music through it right now as I write this chapter. Frankly, in retrospect, I'm not sure that I was ever truly happy before this Christmas.

I'm being a little facetious, of course, at least about being unhappy before getting my iPod. But I am quite serious about the happiness that each of these musical devices has brought me. My guess is that you, too, can think of material goods that you've purchased that have brought you happiness, things that are neither basic survival needs nor luxury items. Cable television or a VCR. A basketball hoop for your driveway. A vacation in the mountains or someplace with a nice beach.

How, then, could it be possible that once people's basic needs have been met—once they are above subsistence incomes—money has almost no impact on their happiness? In my lifetime, I've shifted my music collection from records that scratch and skip to cassette tapes that hiss to CDs that always sound perfect and finally to an iPod that puts more than four thousand selections at my fingertips. In a world where wonderful new technologies abound to those who can afford them, why wouldn't money make people happier?

Is Happiness Relative?

Curious about the small relationship between money and happiness, some economists and psychologists have speculated that relative wealth is a more important determinant of happiness than absolute wealth. To understand the distinction between relative and absolute wealth, imagine that your inflation-adjusted income increases 50 percent over several decades, but all your friends' incomes increase 100 percent. Will you be happy about your increased purchasing power, or will you be bummed out that you are not keeping up with your friends? If happiness is relative, you will not exactly enjoy your increased purchasing power.

Most middle-class families in the United States own material possessions that were beyond the realm of science fiction in the 1940s, contraptions such as color TVs, CD players, and microwave ovens. If absolute wealth were all that mattered, people in the middle class today ought to be happier than people from the upper class fifty years ago, and they ought to be *far* happier than people from the *middle* class fifty years ago. Then again, if relative wealth is what determines happiness, these families will be no happier than middle-class families from the 1950s, because they will still feel deprived compared to others. Their color televisions, superior to any model available during the 1950s, will seem paltry compared to the wide-screen TVs taunting them from the displays at the local Best Buy. Similarly, their 1998 Toyota Camry (far superior to any car built in the 1950s) will seem mundane next to the Lexus passing them on the highway.

How do we find out whether happiness is relative or absolute? Ed Diener and his colleagues tried to find out by looking at happiness and wealth across Americans of different racial groups. Diener predicted that at any given income, African-Americans would be happier than Caucasians because each group would compare themselves to their same-race peers. Diener reasoned that because African-Americans make less money than Caucasians, African-Americans making, say, $60,000 per year would feel relatively wealthier than Caucasians making the same amount and thus would be happier.

The data did not bear out Diener's prediction, however. At any given income level, African-Americans were, in fact, no happier than Caucasians. Being good scientists, Diener and his colleagues did not abandon their theory without further tests, exploring whether the peers people care about are the people in their neighborhoods, rather than some abstract notion of their "racial peers." People with

$60,000 per year incomes, be they African-American or Caucasian, tend to live in neighborhoods where other people make similar incomes. In this case, African-Americans and Caucasians would look down the street and see a bunch of other people making the same incomes they make. Consequently, neither group would feel relatively wealthier than the other. So, Diener and his colleagues analyzed the neighborhoods people lived in. They predicted that among all people with a given income, those who live in relatively poor neighborhoods would be happier than those living in relatively rich ones; people making $60,000 living in a neighborhood where most people make $40,000 will feel relatively rich compared to their neighbors and, thus, will gain more pleasure from their money.

Once again, the data did not bear out Diener's prediction. People relatively poor compared to their neighborhoods were no happier than those who were relatively wealthy.

Does that mean happiness is *not* relative? By no means. For starters, happiness is influenced by many factors which, in combination, could have overwhelmed the factors Diener was studying. For example, imagine a middle-income family living in a low-income neighborhood. Diener predicted this type of family would be happier than the average middle-income family because they would feel wealthy compared to their neighbors. But neighborhoods are more than collections of people to compare oneself to. This family's low-income neighborhood will probably have fewer parks, worse school systems, and higher crime rates than higher income neighborhoods. Isn't it likely that these things overwhelm any joy they receive from being wealthier than their neighbors?

Consider, too, the relationship among race, income, and happiness. Diener predicted that at any given income level, African-Americans would be happier than Caucasians because they would compare themselves to other African-Americans and feel relatively wealthy. But imagine an African-American accountant making $60,000 per year who thinks he would have had an easier time getting promoted if he were not African-American. Rather than thank his lucky stars for making more than many of his racial peers, he might be frustrated that he is not getting promoted as quickly as equally talented Caucasians.

Indeed, as this hypothetical accountant's story suggests, before we accept or dismiss the "happiness is relative" viewpoint, we need to find out *whose* relative wealth people care about. For example, imagine a kindergarten teacher who makes $30,000 per year. When thinking about her salary, does she compare herself to other women? If so, she might be miserable thinking about all the female bankers, doctors, and lawyers who make far more than she does. Does she compare herself to people of her same race? To people of her same race and gender? To people of her same race and gender who live in her neighborhood?

I'm not sure which of these comparisons she would be likely to make. But one comparison seems obvious to me: she will compare herself to other kindergarten teachers. If she is being paid less than similarly talented and experienced teachers, she will be irate. If she is being paid the same amount, she might occasionally wonder why society offers such low wages to kindergarten teachers, but she'll probably harbor little resentment about her low wages.

Hallway Justice

How do any of us know what our employers *ought* to be paying us? By finding out what our peers are being paid. This explains why a baseball player being paid $3 million per year will be unhappy with his salary if he finds out that players with similar batting averages and RBI totals are making $10 million per year. Receive an unexpected $100 bonus, and you will be very happy. Now find out that all your peers received $200 bonuses, and you will be miserable, even though you are still $100 richer than you expected to be. Money brings happiness by allowing us to purchase pleasurable goods. But by acting as a measure of our social worth relative to others, money also brings us pleasure—or displeasure.

In fact, several studies have shown that women are typically happier at any given income than are men, a finding that prompts some experts to conclude that women's happiness depends on their standing relative to other women. As it turns out, however, women don't necessarily compare themselves to other women. Instead, when women are paid less than their work-related peers, they are angry and miserable whether those peers are male or female. In addition, women in predominantly male-dominated professions, whose incomes are higher than the average woman, are not necessarily happier than women in lower-paying jobs. In fact, when they are paid less than their male colleagues, they end up less happy.

Get Used to It

Money doesn't always bring people happiness in the way they think it will. Many of us believe that actress Angelina Jolie has no right to complain when she is paid $2 million less on a film than Julia Roberts, convinced that we'd be happy with the $20 million she takes in. While I have no sympathy for wealthy people who complain about their salaries, I also recognize that their response is very human and quite normal.

In fact, when I read articles by befuddled economists, many of whom find it incomprehensible that money can have so little influence on people's happiness, I start realizing how normal this all is, how normal that money should influence happiness less than people expect. As an expert on the emotional consequences of illness and disability, I have seen the same befuddlement and disbelief among health researchers. And I've conducted studies that demonstrate such disbelief to be misguided. I've come to learn that most people with chronic illness and disability really are as happy as they say.

Adapting to Money

So normal is this relationship between money and happiness that it is explained at least in part by the same phenomenon that explains people's reaction to illness and disability. People adapt! People get used to having what they have, whether it be an above average income or a below-the-knee amputation. You've probably had a friend who bought a new car and washed it every couple of weeks for a while, thrilling to everything about that new vehicle except for the new car smell. But with time, your friend's exuberance likely faded, long before the car's performance began to suffer. Your friend adapted to the car.

This tendency to adapt to good circumstances (such as new cars) would be pretty depressing, except for people's general happiness. I love my iPod (which still hums in my ears right now), but I was pretty happy before my wife gave it to me. While in retrospect I feel like my life was incomplete before I received my iPod, I know these feelings are sorely misguided. iPods are clearly better than Sony Walkmen, which were great improvements over their predecessors. These gadgets improve people's lives, but people's emotions are not geared to experience *sustained* reaction to such gizmos.

My friend George Loewenstein marvels that, despite being such a music buff, I still use the stereo system my sister handed down to me when I was in high school. Undoubtedly my stereo system would sound much better with an infusion of cash. And if anyone would appreciate the wonders of surround sound, it would be me. But Loewenstein also recognizes that I would be happy with just about any kind of stereo system. I'd get used to its sound quality. And my basic nature is unaffected. I'm generally a happy person. How much happier would a subwoofer make me feel?

Do we all spend our lives, then, on hedonic treadmills? Are our emotions immune to circumstance? The answer is no. Most isolated circumstances will have less effect on our emotional lives than we predict. But circumstances can add up, as I'll demonstrate by looking more closely at the relationship between money and happiness among people who experience new adversities.

Does Adversity Alter the Relationship Between Money and Happiness?

To give you an idea of what money can mean in times of adversity, let me tell you about two people at different ends of the income spectrum. The first is a gentleman I took care of two winters ago at the Ann Arbor Veterans Affairs Hospital, who had developed active tuberculosis. His right lung had been almost completely obliterated by the infection; his left lung wasn't far behind. His tuberculosis was highly contagious. Each time he coughed, tubercle bacilli came spewing out of his lungs, clinging onto aerosolized droplets. Anyone breathing this air risked contracting their own case of tuberculosis.

To prevent such contagion, we were forced to put him into an isolation room specially designed to pull air out without circulating it to other parts of the hospital. All visitors, including hospital staff, were required to wear tightly fitting masks whenever they entered this room. Cooped up in this tiny room, this man's days dragged on while he waited for the four antibiotics he was taking to get his infection under control.

Isolation is hard on almost anybody, but it was torture on this man in large part because he was facing major financial problems. Before coming into the hospital, he lived in a trailer home and paid off his bills with the small wage he made slinging burgers at McDonald's. Readers of Barbara Ehrenreich's *Nickel and Dimed* know how hard it is to get by on such wages. He was fortunate to have the VA health system to fall back on so he didn't have to pay large medical bills. But he still needed to pay his rent at the trailer park where he lived, and he wasn't going to be able to do that stuck in a hospital room unable to work.

He paced nervously around the room each day, interrogating us about how much longer we were keeping him in the hospital. His infection was slow to respond to the antibiotics, and the days eventually dragged into weeks. With no family to help him and a girlfriend who had just left him, he couldn't make his trailer payments and was eventually evicted from his home, with his landlord rudely throwing his belongings into the street.

Earlier in this chapter I explained that money matters most for people with very low incomes. As this gentleman's story illustrates, adversity can strike a heavy blow to people living on the financial edge. I never got to know this man well enough to know what his emotional life was like before his illness. But I can tell you with great confidence that his bout with TB took a heavy toll. He eventually made it out of the hospital, leaving with plans to stay at a friend's house until he could find a place to live. But his lungs had been severely damaged, and he still hadn't figured out how he'd get himself back together financially.

The second person I want to tell you about is Scott Mackler, whose financial advantages helped him live with amyotrophic lateral sclerosis (ALS). ALS is a horrifically expensive illness. Fortunately Scott had generous health insurance that has paid many of his expenses. His insurance pays for the computer equipment he uses to communicate to the world as well as the nursing aides he relies on to attend to his frequent needs. Without this insurance coverage, Scott would be dead by now.

Scott's good financial fortune extended beyond his generous health insurance coverage, to include federal grant money to pay for his research. Scott funds his research primarily through National Institutes of Health (NIH) and Veterans Affairs (VA) grants. These granting agencies routinely make additional funds available for investigators who develop disabilities. For example, the grants pay Scott's nursing aide to bring him back and forth to his lab every day as well as to care for him while he works on his research. How many people working at Wal-Mart could find the funds to have a personal nursing aide accompany them to work?

Most important for Scott's quality of life are his own ample financial resources. Scott and Lynn are both successful professionals who have lived a fairly frugal lifestyle, leaving them with more spare change than is available to most families. And despite Scott's illness, both have been able to keep working at jobs that bring them great satisfaction and a fair amount of cash. What's more, early in Scott's illness before he hired a daytime nurse, Lynn's research career gave her the flexibility to work out of Scott's lab. Unlike Ruth Hughes, who lost her job caring for Greg, Lynn was able to supervise the efforts of her many graduate students while staying at Scott's side.

Prior to Scott's illness, I cannot imagine that Scott and Lynn's financial good fortune had much day-to-day impact on their happiness. They adored their boys and loved their careers and had good friends to spend time with. They could have afforded a much larger house than they lived in and could have bought lots of expensive gadgets if they had so desired. But money was not the main focus, or even a major focus, of their lives. ALS has hardly made them into money-obsessed greed mongers, but it has made them much more aware of how important money can be. And it has greatly increased the benefits of being able to afford expensive gadgets. When he turned forty-five two-and-a-half years into his illness, Lynn bought Scott a device that turns the pages of his books for him. The page turner made Scott incredibly happy, allowing him to read books without having to summon help every time he was ready for the next page. Scott's formerly inexpensive obsession with reading had now become an expensive endeavor, but he and Lynn had enough money to continue to feed his habit.

The Buffering Effect of Money

Spurred on by these kinds of stories, I spoke with several colleagues and we decided to find out whether money matters more in people's lives when they confront new illnesses or disabilities. The University of Michigan is headquarters for the Health and Retirement Study, a biannual survey of twenty thousand Americans aged fifty and older that measures, among other things, people's health, wealth, and well-being. We first looked to see whether there was any relationship between wealth and reported happiness among this population. Consistent with the earlier studies I mentioned previously, we found a very slight association between wealth and happiness, with 1 percent of people's happiness accounted for by their life savings. In other words, money didn't play a big role in most people's emotional lives.

Most, but not *all*. You see, over the course of the eight years that the University of Michigan had been collecting data, a number of people participating in the study had become sick or disabled. And, when we looked at these people after the adversity, we found that money was a tenfold better predictor than it had been for the population as a whole. Thus, even though most people remained happy even after becoming sick or disabled, those who had less money had a significantly harder time remaining happy. Their emotional resilience was put through a much harder test.

Another Fundraiser

Scott Mackler did not need to see the results of our study to know how important money was to his emotional well-being. Relatively early in his illness, his close friend Jack Markell asked him what he could do to help him out. Jack had made a decent sized fortune as one of the founders of Nextel and was now the Delaware state treasurer, having dedicated his life to public service. Despite all his money and political connections, however, he felt powerless in the face of Scott's illness. He'd ask Scott what he could do to help and Scott would tell him he just had to stick around and be his friend. "What about a fundraiser to help you deal with this illness?" Jack persisted. Scott quickly rejected that idea, telling Jack he did not need money. "Well, what about raising money for ALS research?" Scott didn't see the point of that either. He could not imagine that a chunk of cash would make much difference in curing ALS in the near future, believing that a cure was more likely to come from advances in basic science than it would from ALS-specific research.

But Jack continued to pester Scott, who finally relented. He had become painfully aware of the financial implications of ALS. He could still work, but most people with ALS could not. He had good disability insurance, but most people did not. And he had personal and family financial resources that were unavailable to most other ALS patients. So Scott decided to let Jack organize a fundraiser, but only on the condition that it be held on behalf of *other* people with ALS.

Scott stipulated that the money be used to provide computers, stair-glides, wheelchairs, wireless doorbell devices, and other contraptions to ALS patients in the greater Philadelphia area. Scott's friends flew from all over the country to attend the fundraiser. In place of an oral speech, Scott presented a slide show using his laptop, with narration provided by a computer program. The slide show was brilliant. It made me laugh; it made my wife cry. At the end of the slide show, Lynn pulled out one of those oversized checks you usually see on TV and revealed that Scott's friends had contributed an unprecedented sum of money to the local ALS association, money that would help hundreds of ALS patients receive the equipment they needed.

Scott has continued to raise money by organizing an annual 5K run to benefit patients with ALS. It must be torture for him to be unable to compete in that race. But he recognizes that his unique intellectual, emotional, and financial resources have helped him find happiness despite his tragic illness, and he wants to give other people those same financial resources to help them in their search for happiness.

The Lessons of Financial Adversity

I don't yet know whether money directly benefits people facing adversity, or whether different types of adversity force people to rely on money more than others. Common sense, however, tells me that money would help most when adversity carries its own financial toll, as it does for people with many illnesses and disabilities. Money also probably comes in handy when people lose their jobs or go through expensive divorces (although I know that money can also be a two-edged sword in this latter situation).

Until the science on money and happiness is worked out in more detail, however, I need to figure out how to live my life. And I have made a few preliminary decisions. I've made sure to get good disability insurance. I've tried not to pursue happiness through material possessions (aside from my iPod of course!). I've worked to save money rather than spend it, and I've refused to even entertain lucrative job offers that would dislocate my family from the community they love.

It makes sense to be prepared for adversity. Some adversities, such as illness and disability, are almost inevitable. Most people develop serious illness or disability at some point in their lives. In preparation for what may come, therefore, I try to watch my finances, careful to remember that my happiness probably depends more on buying an insurance policy to cover a rainy day than on purchasing a vacation home in a place where it doesn't rain.

9

Reassessing Goals in the Face of Adversity

When I was in seventh grade I used to lie in bed pondering infinity. Infinite time, actually—imagining what it would be like to live forever. I envisioned heaven as a place where I could read every good book ever written and then plow through the new books my favorite dead authors had written since they arrived in heaven. I imagined myself spending several hundred years perfecting my bowling game, then spending a few eons working on my free-throw shooting, all the while cognizant that I still had an infinite amount of time to do other things. What made heaven heaven, to me, was all that time.

Now, in my early forties, with a medical career, two young boys, and several neglected hobbies, my belief in an afterlife that includes bowling alleys has diminished—but I am still a huge fan of extra time. There are so many things I would accomplish, I tell myself, if I only had more time. Racing to drop off my kids in time to make it to the clinic by 8:30 A.M., wondering all the while whether I remembered to put the milk back in the refrigerator, I feel like nothing could improve my life more than receiving a couple extra hours each day. And yet, the more I think about time, the less convinced I am that more of it would necessarily make me happier. In fact, I have slowly come to believe that nothing is more detrimental to a well-lived life than having gobs of time.

At least, that is what I believe now, having had the good fortune to get to know a fifty-five-year-old water polo enthusiast named Andy Crawford who had less than one year to live when I met him.

Bone Marrow Transplants and Bangladesh

I first met Andy when he sent me a terse, cryptic e-mail message. "Peter," it began, "I am an engineering professor here at the University"—the University of Michigan where I had taken a job only three months earlier—"and an entrepreneur. I really liked your book *Pricing Life*. I use it in some of my teaching. Due in part to your book, I am using the money I saved by forgoing a bone marrow transplant to start a series of health care clinics in Bangladesh. I'd love to talk with you about it. Andy Crawford."

I read the message several times, unsure what to make of it, especially the connection between his forgone transplant and my book. In *Pricing Life* I had written that expensive medical technology is proliferating so rapidly in the United States that medical clinics and hospitals can no longer afford to offer health care interventions to every patient who could potentially benefit from them. I had urged health care providers instead to spend health care dollars in ways that bring the most important kinds of health benefits and to stop wasting money on medical treatments that have very little chance of benefiting anyone. But nowhere had I specifically written about bone marrow transplants or health care clinics in Bangladesh. Intrigued by his e-mail, I hit the reply key and asked Andy when he could sit down to talk.

Two weeks later I met Andy. I remember feeling as if he had exploded into my office—not because he moved especially fast or talked particularly loud, but because he had such an extraordinary energy about him and such an eagerness to communicate. His energy spilled out into the hallway where I noticed a colleague glancing into my office, wondering who this intense guy was sitting across from me. I closed the door and Andy began telling me his story.

Five years earlier he had been diagnosed with myelofibrosis, a rare disease that was slowly destroying his bone marrow. Myelofibrotic cells were slowly multiplying in his bone marrow cavities, squeezing out the cells that would normally be living there. Because of the myelofibrosis, his bone marrow was increasingly unable to produce red blood cells (the oxygen carrying cells), white blood cells (the infection fighters), and platelets (the little cells that stop bleeding). In response, Andy's spleen had tried to take on the job of producing blood cells, expanding in the process so that instead of being tucked under his left rib cage like normal it now stuck out well below his rib cage. Puffed up like a water balloon, his spleen was one sharp elbow or inadvertent collision away from rupturing, making his oncologist understandably nervous about Andy's thrice-weekly water polo contests.

Until being diagnosed with myelofibrosis, Andy had been the picture of health, which only made it all the more shocking for him to learn that without treatment he had only a handful of years to live. Visiting with Andy in my office that day, I could understand his surprise—Andy did not look like a terminally ill man. Tall and thin, with an athletic demeanor, he was pale because of his profound anemia but otherwise looked healthy. Nevertheless, because of the progression of his illness most weeks he now had two horrible days when the myelofibrosis drained him of all his energy. And he knew the number of miserable days would only get worse. Without treatment, myelofibrosis typically progresses until blood cell and platelet transfusions lose their effectiveness (because people build up immunities to transfusions, rejecting the transfused cells shortly after they are infused) or until serious infections intervene (because myelofibrosis thwarts white blood cell production). "At some point, my good days will be too rare to make life worth living. When that happens," he told me, "I will kill myself." He told me about his suicide plan less than five minutes after we met. Andy was not exactly shy.

But he was not visiting me to tell me about his illness. Instead, he wanted to tell me what he was doing now that he had developed this illness. He told me how—at least on days in which he felt reasonably energetic—he was busy teaching an undergraduate course on entrepreneurship, helping the University of Michigan Health System raise money for an Integrative Medicine and Healing Center, and starting a series of health care clinics in Bangladesh.

As I got to know Andy better, I realized that he was not pursuing these activities despite his illness but *because* of it. Faced with a death sentence, Andy Crawford decided to take advantage of his intellectual, emotional, and financial resources and pour his remaining energy into causes he cared passionately about. When Andy realized he had no more than five years to live, he responded with a burst of urgent energy. He could no longer live as if death was a distant reality. The time to act was now, and, as a result, Andy decided he had better get moving if he was going to have any chance to leave his mark on the world.

How Would You Spend $100,000?

As we visited that first day, Andy explained the connection between his bone marrow transplant and Bangladesh with impenetrable logic. Shortly after receiving his diagnosis, Andy learned everything he could about myelofibrosis, scouring books, surfing the Internet, and harassing physician friends for information. When hope for a cure eluded him, he traveled to the Mayo Clinic for a final opinion to see if they had new treatments to offer. He met with Dr. Ayalew Tefferi, a hematologist whom I remembered as an excellent clinician from my days training at Mayo a decade earlier. Tefferi was remarkably candid, telling Andy his only chance of survival was a bone marrow transplant but at his age—Andy was in his mid-fifties—the chance was only one in ten. Andy contemplated his alternatives. Ten percent odds did not sound very good, but 10 percent was a lot larger than 0 percent, and Andy had always been an overachiever. And he was much healthier than most fifty-five-year-olds. If anyone could beat the odds, it would be Andy.

But Andy did not think it was a justifiable gamble. Bone marrow transplants, he reminded me, cost well over $100,000. "Just like you wrote about in your book, rather than buying a bone marrow transplant with only a 10 percent chance of saving my life, that $100,000 could be used to save thousands of lives if spent more wisely." He explained that a college friend of his wife's ran a Boston charity that had established a large health care presence in Bangladesh. "A $100,000 donation to the charity could provide health care for ten thousand garment workers over the next year," he pointed out.

I was confused. His insurance company was willing to pay $100,000 or more for a bone marrow transplant, but surely it was not willing to take that same amount of money and give it to this charity. "Of course it won't," Andy said. "But that is not the point. You see, it *would* have spent $100,000 or more on me if I had chosen a transplant, and that makes no sense to me. That amount of money could do so much more good. So I decided to spend $100,000 of my *own* money to jump-start this Bangladesh project."

The Relationships Between Goals and Happiness

It was shortly before I met Andy that I began to study the secrets of emotional resilience—the gap between how people think they will feel if they experience an adversity like a chronic illness and the way they *actually* feel in such circumstances. No situation seems as impervious to emotional resilience as being diagnosed with a fatal illness. Indeed, the best-known description of how people deal with fatal illnesses, Elizabeth Kubler-Ross's ground-breaking book *On Death and Dying*, paints a gloomy picture of people proceeding through various stages—of denial, anger, bargaining, and depression, none of these being happiness-filled stages—all in a hope that they will attain a final stage of acceptance, a stage Kubler-Ross describes as being almost devoid of emotion. To most people, terminal illness conjures images of grief, anger, and, at best, resignation. One never thinks of being *energized* by death—of fifty-five-year-old men who in the face of death decide to do something to change the world, to dramatically influence thousands of lives.

People underestimate their own emotional resilience in part because they don't realize the important role that goal-setting plays in helping people find happiness. Numerous studies show that people who set clear goals for themselves are happier than those who do not. What's more, people who pursue intrinsically motivated goals are happier than those who pursue extrinsically motivated ones. For example, college students who study or engage in extracurricular activities because they enjoy learning or playing sports are happier than those who study or play sports in order to please their parents or to get into a good graduate school.

"Ideal" Goals Versus "Ought" Goals

Happiness depends in part, then, on whether people pursue intrinsic or extrinsic goals. Happiness also depends on whether people strive for *ideal* goals—high aspirations, such as the goal I pursue of learning and mastering every Beethoven sonata, a goal I will never meet because mastery of such music is beyond my abilities—versus *ought* goals—minimum standards people set for themselves, such as, "I'd better do at least this well or I will be disappointed."

Consider Michelle Kwan's performances in the 2000 and 2002 winter Olympics, in which she was the favorite each time to win a gold medal in women's figure skating. In both Olympiads, she entered the final evening of competition in the lead but then skated tentatively, trying desperately to avoid a mistake that would lose her the gold medal she was expected to win. And in both Olympiads, she *did* lose the gold medal, each time to a sixteen-year-old whose goal had simply been to skate the best program of her life. There is a big difference between setting "ought" goals (I want to avoid falling on my triple axel) and "ideal" goals (I want to perform the most explosive yet graceful triple axel in history).

Ought goals are often negative—the ultimate endpoint is for something *not* to happen; a basketball player tries not to miss the game-winning free throw. Ideal goals are more positive; a basketball player stands on the free-throw line determined to touch nothing but net. People generally enjoy the positive pursuit of ideal goals more than the negative pursuit of ought goals. Consequently, they often accomplish much more when pursuing ideal goals. Moreover, people react very differently to the achievement of ideal versus ought goals. When people achieve their ideal goals, they are very happy; when they achieve ought goals, they are relieved but not necessarily happy.

My free-throw analogy may seem spurious. Logically speaking, there is no difference between making a free throw and not missing an attempted free throw, but psychologically, ideal and ought goals are very different. For example, most people think more favorably of a surgical procedure with a 90 percent survival rate than a procedure with a 10 percent mortality rate. Strange, I know, but nevertheless true. Still don't believe that positive and negative framing matters? Try telling a toddler to stop standing in the bathtub. Now ask the same toddler if he can show you how well he can sit down in the bathtub. Guess which approach brings better results!

The Refocusing Power of Adversity

It seems obvious that pursuing intrinsically enjoyable and meaning-ful goals will make people happy. But many people are unaware that they have let themselves get into a goal rut. It is easy for people—once they finish school, get married, and settle into a job—to stop focusing on anything but extrinsically meaningful goals. Which is precisely why adversity can make people happy; like very few things, adversity has the power to refocus people's attention on deciding what they really want to do with their lives.

When my research team has asked healthy people to think about serious illness, like kidney failure, people imagine being forced to give up their careers and to abandon their favorite hobbies. In these respects, their imaginations are accurate. Only a small percentage of patients with kidney failure are able to hold down full-time jobs and, because of the demands of attending dialysis sessions three days per week, many are forced to abandon favorite pastimes like traveling. But healthy people's imaginations fail to grasp that people can shift their life goals to account for the limitations imposed on them by their illnesses. They overlook the possibility that people will no longer require full-time jobs to feel fulfilled by their work, or that people will find new hobbies to replace the old ones they have been forced to abandon.

In fact, in response to chronic illness, many people shift their life goals almost subconsciously. Early in my clinical career, I remember being surprised by some of my patients with emphysema who, despite severe damage to their lungs, rarely complained of being short of breath. Then one day I asked a particularly happy patient, whose lung function was less than a quarter of normal, how often he experienced shortness of breath. "Never," he told me. "What about walking upstairs or carrying groceries in from the car?" I asked. "Those activities don't make me short of breath," he said. I looked at him incredulously for a moment before he rebutted my skepticism. "Those activities don't make me short of breath," he explained, "because I don't *do* those activities."

This man was not bothered by his lung disease, because he had abandoned the kinds of activities that would make him short of breath. This abandonment had occurred so gradually, over so many years, that he barely noticed how much he had given up. He told me how he had always loved taking long walks outdoors, but that his walks had gradually gotten shorter and shorter until he stopped doing them. He abandoned walking over such a long period of time that he never noticed the change in his lifestyle.

Changing Life Goals in the Face of Reality

Serious illness and disability often force people to change their goals to fit their new circumstances. This is not an automatic process. For example, men who undergo treatment for prostate cancer often experience troublesome side effects, like impotence and incontinence. Not surprisingly, men who experience such side effects are generally less happy than those who do not. But these side effects primarily reduce happiness in men whose life goals do not change.

In those men who change their goals to account for their new circumstances, such side effects have no net effect on their happiness; in fact, they are happier than they were before their prostate cancer treatment, as if the cancer (and accompanying side effects) has helped them reset their life priorities. Similarly, some people with AIDS place a high value on health-related goals, such as slowing the progression of their disease or avoiding as much pain as possible, while others have nonhealth-related goals, such as spending time with friends and family. And as these people become sicker, it is the people in the former group who suffer the most emotionally, unless they shift their priorities to nonhealth-related goals.

Though illness can force people to abandon goals, most people with chronic illnesses still manage to find happiness. They find it not because they ignore the ways their lives have changed, but because they consciously or subconsciously begin to find meaning in those parts of their lives unaffected by illness. By being forced to abandon normal day-to-day activities, people begin to think seriously about what pursuits will fill their lives with the greatest sense of meaning and purpose.

Andy Crawford was not aimlessly wandering through an unfulfilled life before illness struck. Even before he became sick, he had always been goal-directed. Perpetually energetic and optimistic, he had built a successful T-shirt business and had patented several technologies that enabled customers to design and print their own T-shirts. In fact, two years before Andy became sick he had begun working long hours trying to expand his business online. Then, illness stepped in and dramatically reshaped his goals.

But it was not Andy who first became sick. His wife, Karen, was diagnosed with breast cancer first. After Karen's diagnosis, Andy wanted to spend more time with her, to help her think through her breast cancer treatment options. He took time off work and filled the Crawford household with flipcharts and diagrams so he could help her sort through her treatment alternatives. Later, Andy reduced his work hours even further to help Karen fight through her treatment and its side effects.

When Andy himself became sick two years later, he altered his life goals once again, focusing his remaining years on charitable work and teaching. Andy's personality did not change when he became sick. He remained as energetic and optimistic as ever, and his way of pursuing goals did not change either. As always, he pursued goals he cared about with focus and intensity. What changed were the kinds of goals that he cared about.

With only a few more years to live, Andy could not muster much enthusiasm for T-shirt entrepreneurship. Instead, he threw his business talents into his Bangladesh project.

True to his entrepreneurial spirit, once Andy turned his attention to supporting medical clinics in Bangladesh, he wondered why he should settle for providing health care to Bangladeshis for only a single year. Wouldn't it make more sense, he asked himself, to build a sustainable health care program that could provide health care indefinitely? Determined to have a longer lasting effect, Andy got together with his son, Alex, a former documentary filmmaker and journalist, to start a group of health care clinics in Bangladesh that would be self-sustaining.

Interested in learning more about the Bangladesh project, I met with Andy and Alex over lunch several weeks after my first meeting with Andy. "I want to do something with my dad before he dies," Alex said, between bites of his sandwich. "I had a bunch of ideas for start-up companies but none of that appealed to my dad's idealistic side. I'm cynical, which you kind of have to be when you are a journalist. But my dad really thinks he can save the world—or at least make it a better place. So the Bangladesh project seemed like a good opportunity for us to work together."

A filmmaker/journalist may seem like a strange person to help start a health care program in Bangladesh, even if he is your son. But Alex is not your typical filmmaker. He has the expected ponytail and tattoos, but they come off less like fashion accessories and more like symbols of a rough-lived life. He specializes in exploring what his dad describes as "the extremes of life on this planet." One of Alex's documentaries featured a punk rock band who was known for performing in the nude. Another focused on Al Goldstein, America's first "great" pornographer, according to Alex, whose battles with the FBI throughout the 1970s opened the marketplace for upstart competitors such as Larry Flynt, the founder of *Hustler* magazine. More recently, Alex interviewed militants on all sides of the struggles in Northern Ireland. Experiences such as these have made Alex quite comfortable dealing with people from all walks of life.

This background prepared him well for the corruption, guile, and strong-arming that he encountered upon traveling to Bangladesh. "Make a contract with a local government operator or builder to put up a health care clinic and they will subcontract part of the work to another group, who in turn will sub-subcontract some other portion of that work to another group, with each contract, subcontract, and sub-subcontract eating up some portion of the revenues. In most cases, the contractor, the subcontractor, and the sub-subcontractor are really the same people, who make shell companies to hide their identities." Through this kind of corruption, a $100,000 investment in a medical clinic might lead to only $10,000 of real work.

Feeling that the charity organization was not capable of bypassing the corruption as well as he was, Alex decided to build health care clinics without the help of the Boston charity that he and Andy had initially planned to work with. Andy interjected from across the table. "But you know, Alex, the Boston charity funds over 150 medical clinics in Bangladesh." "Yeah, Dad, but five other charities think they are solely responsible for funding the *same* 150 medical clinics." Andy looked incredulous. Alex began to get worked up. "Do you even begin to realize the kind of people we are dealing with here, Dad? You are simply too naive. You're too idealistic to see what is happening!"

I felt like I had an inkling of what dinners at the Crawford residence must have been like when Alex was growing up.

A Sisyphean Task?

According to Greek legend, Sisyphus, father of Odysseus, was condemned in the underworld to push a huge stone up a steep hill. But each time he attempted the task, the stone always rolled down before he reached the top and Sisyphus was forced to begin all over again.

The gods figured there was no better way to punish Sisyphus than to condemn him to an eternity of futile and hopeless labor. In *The Myth of Sisyphus*, Albert Camus takes this legend as a metaphor for the absurdity of life, which he says arises out of a confrontation between the human need for meaning and "the unreasonable silence of the world." Camus envisions Sisyphus as the absurd hero because he continues to have passion for life despite his eternally futile pursuit:

> One sees the face screwed up, the cheek tight against the stone, the shoulder bracing the clay covered mass, the foot wedging, the fresh start with arms outstretched, the wholly human security of two earth-clotted hands. At the very end of his long effort measured by skyless space and time without depth, the purpose is achieved. Then Sisyphus watches the stone rush down in a few moments toward that lower world whence he will have to push it up again toward the summit. He goes back down to the plain.
>
> It is during that return, that pause, that Sisyphus interests me . . . that hour like a breathing space which returns as surely as his suffering, that is the hour of consciousness. At each of those moments when he leaves the heights and gradually sinks toward the lairs of the gods, he is superior to his fate. He is stronger than his rock.

After hearing Alex describe his travels to Bangladesh, I could not help but think that Andy and Alex's Bangladesh efforts were Sisyphean. Except the rock doesn't roll down the hill passively. Each time they try pushing the rock up the hill, a bunch of corrupt people stand on the other side *pushing* it back down.

Is this how Andy wants to spend his hard-earned money, not to mention the last months of his life? "Sure," he said. "It may not

work, but at least I will have tried." Being given a death sentence
had focused Andy's already prodigious energies, even as myelofibrosis sapped him of some of his physical strength.

Rather than become defeated by his diagnosis, Andy has turned
it into an inspiration; rather than become depressed, he is having the
time of his life. He loves working on the project. It gives him an
excuse to work with Alex and to work with students, whom he can
inspire to commit themselves to the pursuit of social justice. As
much as he hopes to establish clinics in Bangladesh, the political,
social, and intellectual challenge is in itself pleasurable.

The Death Sentences We All Face

Several weeks after my lunch with Andy and Alex, I arranged to
meet Andy again to learn more about his Bangladesh project. However, in typical fashion, I failed to confirm the time and location of
our lunch and found myself sitting alone in one of Ann Arbor's most
popular restaurants. Feeling awkward, I ordered a beer and took out
my scratch paper, pretending I was a great thinker who had come to
the restaurant alone on purpose. Inspired by Andy, I started jotting
down notes about what I would do if I were given an imminent
death sentence. I drew three columns down a piece of scratch paper.
In one column, I wrote down what I would do if I had twenty-four
hours to live. In another I wrote down what I would do if I had a
month to live. And in a third column, I pondered what I would do
with the last year of my life.

At the top of the page I wrote "Books" and began pondering
what books I would read if I had a year to live. I began this way
because Andy told me at our first meeting that he no longer read
fiction, as if his impending death made make-believe an unafford-
able luxury. With a year to live, would I make any time for light fic-

tion or would I have time for only "serious" books? Or would it be too late for anything serious, like at bedtime when I push the *New England Journal* aside in favor of the local sports section? What piano pieces would I practice if I had only one month to live? Would I learn any new music? Would I even bother playing piano, with so many things I could do instead to improve the world?

I felt like I was stuck in one of those inane childhood conversations about whether you would rather be blind or deaf. Except my jottings in no way felt inane or useless. Rather, by reflecting on the unimaginable, I was hoping to improve the way I lived my life. Andy's disease forced him to have this conversation with himself, and it forced his son to find a way to spend more time with him. Maybe if I asked myself these questions, I would live my own life more wisely, spending more time improving the world, say, and less time watching "SportsCenter."

As I sat alone nursing my beer and jotting down notes about what I would do if I had twenty-four hours to live, Andy and his family were discussing the exact same questions in a University of Michigan hospital room. Andy missed our lunch not because I had screwed up the scheduling but because his slowly progressive bone marrow failure had transformed into an acute leukemia. Some type of genetic switch had flipped, and Andy's myelofibrotic cells, rather than satisfying themselves by ploddingly reproducing in his bone marrow, began producing hundreds of thousands of white blood cells that literally overwhelmed Andy's body. Andy's platelet count was desperately low, and his body was violently rejecting platelet transfusions, leaving him vulnerable to internal bleeding. If he bled into his brain, he would die instantly.

Things were so tenuous, in fact, that in his lucid moments, when the morphine levels came down a bit, Andy was trying to figure out what to do with his remaining hours, days, or weeks. If the leukemia did not settle down soon, Andy would be dead within a day or two. Which people would he want to see? What final tasks would he wrap up and what would he leave unattended?

Fortunately, over the next few days, Andy's leukemia responded to medications, and he was able to go home. I visited him there a week later. My doctor instincts were on high alert. He was thinner and paler than when I had last seen him. His breathing was shallow. He told me he had leukemic cells in the lining of his heart that made it difficult for him to take a deep breath.

Nevertheless, he seemed upbeat and was eager to tell me what was going on in his life. "The oncologist told me I had three treatment alternatives for my leukemia," he said. "The first treatment is a medicine called Hydrea. This temporarily slows down the leukemia, but almost no one on Hydrea lives more than three months. The second treatment is an aggressive chemotherapy that would make me miserable for a month, force me to spend another month recovering, and probably add about three months to my life—if it doesn't kill me right away. Easy decision there, just like the bone marrow transplant, I don't see that as being worthwhile. The final option is an experimental protocol that even the oncologist thinks is a long shot. So I'm choosing Hydrea and hoping to pull some things together over the next couple of months, rather than grasp at some nonexistent straws."

What exactly was he hoping to pull together, I wondered? "I'm busy working on three-and-a-half projects," he said with characteristic precision. "First, I'm trying to push along the development of an integrative medicine center at the university. One goal of the new center is to study the role of alternative medicines in the care of dying patients. The last couple weeks have really shown me how important that is." Andy then described his other projects. "Second, I'm trying to push along my Bangladesh project. Third, I'm planning my memorial service. And the half-project I'm working on is to help a professor take over my entrepreneurship class. I'm trying to help him interpret my class notes."

Unfortunately, because of side effects from his medications, it was difficult for Andy to make progress on these three-and-a-half projects. But he was optimistic that his productivity would increase over the next few weeks. "I'm constantly adjusting my medicines to find the right balance between symptom relief and alertness. It is already better than it was a couple days ago. The hospital stay wiped me out, but I am already beginning to feel more energetic."

With less than three months to live, Andy still exuded optimism. He had accepted his fate but not passively and not without a sense of urgency to accomplish as much as possible over the next three months. Always obsessed with goals, Andy went on to tell me he asks students in his entrepreneurship class to write down their major life goals. Where do they want to be in twenty years? What will they want to have accomplished? And unlike many entrepreneurship classes, he did not let them focus on career goals but made them think about their family goals, hobbies, and community activities. Planning a career is impossible, he taught them, without thinking about these other goals. Andy used his entrepreneurship class to teach students how to plan their lives, not just their business pursuits.

As he told me about his entrepreneurship class, I sensed he was trying to teach me, too. I don't think Andy could stop himself from wanting to mentor people. In fact, the first time we had met, Andy had asked me about the research program I was building. Upon learning about my program, he immediately offered his help. When I thanked him politely, he was not satisfied. He took another moment to think about *how* he could help me. He ticked off a list of people he would introduce me to who would help me build my research program. Visiting with him now in his house as his death approached, I sensed that the same forces were at work. Andy was the type of teacher who wanted to help people accomplish their goals and hoped to teach them something about life on the way.

Andy's Momentum

A week after visiting Andy at his home, I asked him if we could get together again. He told me it was not a good week—he was undergoing localized radiation therapy to control pain from his leukemia. A week later, his wife, Karen, sent an e-mail letting me know the end was near. Andy's blood counts were so low his doctors were stunned he was even alive and getting around. His energy was waning, and a transfusion did little to improve matters. Andy went off his chemotherapy and finished tidying up his affairs. He stayed in bed most of the time for his last few days, visiting with family while awake and ultimately dying peacefully in his sleep.

Andy's memorial service was jammed with friends, relatives, colleagues, and students. Among the crowd was David Moore, a marketing professor whose daughter, Elisa, had been one of Andy's students and decided to get involved in his Bangladesh project. Andy had inspired her to become more interested in community service and international justice. Indeed, she had shown signs of Andy-like energy. In between classes, she had somehow found the time to learn Portuguese, travel to Brazil, volunteer for Al Gore's presidential campaign, and start a campus ministry for Seventh Day Adventists who were attending the University of Michigan. Then, tragedy intervened. Returning from the polls after voting for Gore, Elisa was killed in a car accident.

David met Andy when Andy spoke at Elisa's memorial service and quickly realized why his daughter had been so inspired by him. Six months after Elisa's death, David met with Andy to discuss an idea—he wanted to start a scholarship fund in memory of his daughter. Andy loved the idea and quickly gave him his first donation. But in the five months since meeting with Andy, David's work on the scholarship fund had stalled. As much as he wanted to do something in Elisa's memory, David found that working on the scholarship fund kept dredging up painful feelings.

After attending Andy's memorial service, David finally overcame his inertia. "So many people at the memorial service spoke about how much Andy had inspired them," he told me, "that I realized I needed to get back to work if for no other reason than to keep from disappointing Andy in his grave." He explained how the memorial service motivated him to do something to honor his daughter. "I pass within forty feet of Elisa's grave each day when I drive to work. I do not want her memory relegated to a highly polished tombstone."

Within three weeks of Andy's memorial service, David had pulled everything together and gotten the scholarship fund up and running. In a turn of logic inspired by Andy, David realized that because college was so expensive in the United States, a scholarship fund would have to be incredibly well endowed to have any impact. A native of Trinidad, he realized that money would go much further elsewhere. "The scholarship fund will help young women who want to enroll in the Caribbean Union College. I hope soon to have enough money that we can award a new scholarship annually."

Dying for Several Decades

In continuing to study the relationship between health and happiness, I have frequently found myself thinking about Andy. Faced with a terminal illness, Andy was hardly eager to die, but neither was he afraid to die. He accepted his fate and proceeded to make the most of his remaining days. He made sure to spend quality time with Karen and Alex, but he did not retreat into his family shell. Rather, he responded to his cancer diagnosis by turning his energy outward. Andy was always a natural leader and a talented teacher.

Cancer simply increased his desire to lead and teach. And never were his unique talents more on display than when Andy learned he was dying.

Myelofibrosis brought the best out in Andy in part because, until the very end, it did not take away his energy or his ability to pursue the goals he cared about. In that respect, Andy was lucky because terminal illnesses are not always so kind. But I also expect myelofibrosis brought out the best in Andy because it gave him a lengthy, but finite, amount of time to establish and pursue his last few goals. If upon learning of his illness he had been told that he had only three months to live, I expect that Andy would have attended to family affairs and urgent business matters. But told he had five years to live—now, that was a time span he could make use of!

Five years was enough time for Andy to pursue ambitious goals, while still filling him with a sense of urgency. It was long enough to force him to think about what he would do with the rest of his life, and short enough to focus his energy on only those goals he cared about the most. Andy's five-year death sentence, tragic as it was to receive at such a young age, was also a gift.

Given too much time, it is easy to let life slip away. We grow up, expecting to live to a ripe old age, and let precious moments slip by without taking advantage of them. The Talking Heads have a beautiful song in which David Byrne languorously sings about heaven as a place where "nothing, . . . nothing ever happens." My seventh-grade view of heaven, as an infinitely enjoyable bowling alley, has shifted much closer to Byrne's view. Given infinite time to perfect my bowling game, why would I feel any rush to practice today? Given so much time I could practically do nothing and still reach my goal, eventually, of bowling a perfect game.

Too much time is a curse. Too much free time and we see no reason not to sit and watch "The Brady Bunch" reruns. Think of all those people who enter into retirement excited to finally have time to pursue all their favorite hobbies, only to find out instead that retirement leaves them with too much free time, which they then fritter away until they wonder where the years have gone.

Andy has made me think about what I can do to maximize my impact on other people. I cannot do all the things Andy was able to do. I do not have the leadership skills and entrepreneurial talents to start up health care clinics in Third World countries. And I have young children at home, with whom I want to spend gobs of time. Nevertheless, Andy said my previous book had inspired him to begin his Bangladesh project. And so, in a nice piece of symmetry, Andy ended up inspiring me to write this book.

I often think of Andy when I lie in bed at 5 A.M. trying to decide whether or not to sneak downstairs to write. Thinking of Andy often encourages me to get out of bed. I am dying after all, but hopefully not for a handful of decades. And during that time, I hope to live my life with enough sense of imminent death to focus my energy on pursuing meaningful goals, the way Andy did when he decided to forgo that potentially lifesaving bone marrow transplant.

10

Religious Beliefs and Spirituality During Times of Adversity

A half-dozen years after being diagnosed with his chordoma, Jay Schreiner received what seemed like a run of the mill invitation from his priest. "I'd like you and M.B. to come to mass thirty minutes early this Sunday," he said. "I want to show you some remodeling work we are doing in the rectory." Father Victor's request was not at all out of the ordinary. Jay and M.B. had been coming to his church for several years and had become good friends with him. In addition, Jay never turned down an opportunity to see how someone was fixing something up. He loved to fix things up around his house and eagerly came to church early that day to see what size joists Father Victor was using.

Sunday mass began at 10:00 A.M., so Jay and M.B. arrived at the church around 9:30. Father Victor greeted them enthusiastically at the door and brought them back behind the sacristy. Then his expression became more serious; he confessed that he had brought them there under false pretenses. He was not remodeling the rectory and had no joists for them to look at. Instead, he hoped to take this thirty-minute opportunity to offer Jay and M.B. the sacrament of matrimony. Jay and M.B. had already married each other in a Methodist ceremony, and since then M.B. had converted to Roman Catholicism, to the chagrin of her evangelical parents. But she and

Jay had been unable to receive a Roman Catholic wedding because Jay had not yet annulled his first marriage.

Father Victor explained that under special circumstances, such as during wartime or at time of impending death, Roman Catholic priests are allowed to offer the sacrament of matrimony to people even if they have not gone through a lengthy annulment process. He did not elaborate on these details, which made Jay and M.B. suspicious that Father Victor had been goaded into this action by Father John, a retired priest in the parish—a man filled with warmth and love who was not known for being the most strict follower of canon law. Jay was undergoing his fifth round of neurosurgery the next day, in what looked like the riskiest operation to date. The chordoma was encroaching on a major blood vessel to Jay's brain and on a vital portion of his spinal cord. There was a real chance he would suffer a debilitating stroke or an irreversible spinal cord injury. Jay's surgery was just the type of circumstance that eliminated the need for an annulment, Father Victor said, as he reiterated his offer to marry them right then and there, if they were interested.

Interested?! They leapt at the opportunity. When Jay first learned that he had a chordoma, he and M.B. had put aside any idea of annulling Jay's first marriage. They didn't want to waste any of their limited emotional energy on an annulment when they might have so little time together. Religion was an important part of their lives, and Our Lady of Consolation was an important part, too. They'd simply come to expect that they would not be married in the Roman Catholic Church any time soon. So they enthusiastically accepted Father Victor's kind offer, and he married them on the spot, in plenty of time for them to sink into their usual pew for the 10:00 A.M. mass, with strangely euphoric looks on their faces.

Jay has told me a number of times that religion has played an important role in his battle with cancer, attributing much of his emotional strength to the faith he shares with M.B. And Jay is not alone in finding strength through his religion. Religion is a consistent predictor of happiness in many studies. And studies have shown that people with strong religious faith typically bounce back from adversity more quickly and more thoroughly than others. Religion, it seems, is good emotional medicine.

Religious Life Is Both Public and Private

So far in this chapter, I've thrown around religion pretty loosely, without clarifying whether I'm referring to people's affiliations with specific religious organizations or instead to their private beliefs and practices regardless of whether such beliefs and practices conform to any official organization. To some people, religion connotes highly structured, hierarchical organizations. Some people, in fact, believe it is possible to be religious ("I go to church every Sunday") without being spiritual (" . . . but I never pray and only go to church out of habit"). Other people believe that religion involves a set of beliefs and practices that influence a person's life independent of any community organization they belong to. Take a trip to California and you are likely to run into someone who says, "I am not religious at all, but I am very spiritual!" In this chapter, unless I specify otherwise, I will use the term *religion* to include both participation in public religious organizations and private spiritual experiences.

So, what is it about religious life that bolsters people's emotional resilience? Jay would hardly know where to begin to explain why his Roman Catholic faith has meant so much to him these past ten years. For starters, he has made many good friends through his church, and, as I discussed earlier, Jay is as much of a people person as I have had the pleasure to meet in my life. He simply loves interacting with people and looks forward, every Sunday, to meeting up with the parishioners he has gotten to know at St. Mary's. Indeed, after each of his operations Jay measures his recovery by seeing how quickly he can make it back to Sunday mass.

To many people, in fact, the social aspects of religious experience loom particularly large in their lives. Religious organizations are a great source of friends—not just any friends, but friends who often hold common beliefs about what is important in life. In addition, religious communities often come together to help those among them who are sick. Religious participation can also help people fit into their social communities. Being Mormon in Utah is a good thing, socially speaking, making it much easier to meet people without fear of being ostracized.

The social benefits of religious practice are so substantial that some religious communities verge on being social clubs rather than spiritual organizations, clubs where people focus on discussing and sharing their values. Many Unitarian churches in the United States, for example, have essentially become institutions for secular humanists. A Sunday morning at such an institution may pass by without mention of God, but with much sharing of family values.

Although Jay Schreiner clearly appreciates the social aspects of his Roman Catholic practice, he treasures the more spiritual aspects of his faith, too. Jay has suffered immensely over the past decade, experiencing more pain than most people will encounter in their lifetime. He has wondered, many times, why he was stricken with a chordoma. Some days he shrugs it off as bad luck. But other days he takes some solace in the idea that it is part of God's plan. When he suffers from pain, he offers his suffering up to God. When he feels like pitying himself, he turns to his faith to remind himself of his many blessings.

Bringing Meaning and Purpose to Suffering

When people suffer from adversity, religious beliefs can boost their emotional resilience by giving meaning and purpose to their suffering. At an extreme, religious beliefs can help people by giving them hope that their suffering will be rewarded in the afterlife. Aware of how well religious belief relieved suffering, Karl Marx complained bitterly that religion minimized the pain people felt at the hands of an unfair capitalist system, thereby preventing them from improving their lives. Marx was upset because he believed people were suffering needlessly due to the greedy ruthlessness of people with fiscal capital. But sometimes suffering is unavoidable and cannot be cured by a political revolution or by a round of chemotherapy. Jay's pain, for example, is simply a part of his life. Whatever rewarding properties his religious life has brought him over the past ten years, I hardly think it would deserve Marx's ire.

Jay's religious life not only provides him with social capital, so to speak, and with a sense that his suffering has meaning, but it also provides him with the special power of prayer. Take away Jay's church and he still would have prayer. And with prayer, Jay is able to find peace of mind. He's able to take time to be thankful for the many ways he has been blessed while asking for help to meet the many challenges he faces.

Jay is a religious man, but he is not a zealot. He doesn't wear his faith on his sleeve, neither proselytizing nor preaching to those who don't share his faith. But when asked about his illness, he is quite upfront that he doesn't believe he could have made it through the past decade without the strength of his faith.

Religion, Spirituality, and Emotional Resilience

Jay's experience reveals that religion influences people's emotional lives in many ways, by encouraging important social interactions as well as promoting private behaviors such as prayer. Which of these aspects of religion promote emotional resilience?

Sociologist Melvin Pollner used data from a large survey to explore the relationship between religiousness and happiness. He found that the more religious people were, the happier they were. Aware of the richness of religious experience, he looked separately at the internal and external aspects of religious experience and found that both were associated with how happy people were.

In another fine study, sociologist Christian Ellison divided religious experience into three aspects: religious attendance, personal relationships with God (through activities like prayer), and what he called "existential certainty." Existential certainty is measured by asking people whether they have any religious doubts and whether external circumstances raised any questions in their minds about the meaning and purpose of life. He found that this last aspect of religion, existential certainty, was also strongly associated with people's overall life satisfaction. People who are certain that life has meaning and purpose are happier than others.

Studies like these suggest that religious beliefs and practice are associated with happiness. But they do not establish cause and effect. In other words, there are no studies that show that religious people are happier than nonreligious ones. Both Pollner and Ellison collected data about people's religiousness at the same time that they inquired about their happiness. Their studies, therefore, cannot determine whether religion makes people happy, or, instead, whether happy people are simply more likely to find religion than unhappy people.

Which Comes First—Religiousness or Happiness?

One way to sort out cause and effect is to study people across time, to see whether religiousness precedes happiness, or vice versa. People's religious beliefs change over the course of their lives, for example. What happens to their happiness when they become more or less religious? As it turns out, studies of people who undergo religious conversions show them to become more happy after their conversions. This evidence does not convince most experts that religion causes happiness, however, because it raises questions about why these people underwent religious conversions. Were they having specific crises at the time? If so, were they inevitably going to become happier over time, once the crises had abated, whether or not they found religion?

One of the most compelling studies I have read not only does a convincing job of showing that religious experience can precede happiness but also shows the special importance religion can take on in people's lives during times of adversity. In the study, Ellen Idler, a health-care researcher at Rutgers University, followed a group of elderly people in New Haven, Connecticut. In her initial survey, Idler measured public and private components of religion, including religious affiliation, attendance at services, and depth of religiosity. Over the next five years, she assessed how healthy and happy people were. She discovered that all people who developed new disabilities over that time period became more likely to get depressed, but that those with strongly held private religious beliefs were less prone to such depression. By following these people over time, Idler didn't have to worry that people became religious in order to cope with their disabilities or that happy people gravitated more toward religion after becoming disabled than did unhappy people. She knew, instead, that being religious at the beginning of the time period helped people avoid depression after they developed disabilities.

The Lessons of Religious Life for Religious and Nonreligious People

These studies are scientifically important because they help answer whether or how religion contributes to people's emotional resilience. But they are also important because they serve as reminders about how we can all bolster our emotional resilience. It helps to remember the many ways that religious experience functions. Some people may attend religious services regularly without setting aside much time the rest of the week to pray. These people's emotional resilience would probably be stronger if they attended to the full range of their religious experience.

Similarly, some people with deeply practiced spiritual lives may nevertheless benefit from partaking more in the social aspects of their religious lives. In fact, based on what I discussed in Chapter 6, about the benefits of helping others, in times of adversity many religious people might do well to perform church-related volunteer work. Religious organizations provide many opportunities for people to help others. For our own sakes, we should take advantage of such opportunities.

But the lessons of these scientific studies are not limited to people with strongly held religious beliefs. Indeed, many benefits of religion are available to people regardless of their belief system. For example, people who attend religious services are typically happier than those who do not. Religious services promote valuable social activity and motivate people to get out of the house. But other social activities as well as other community organizations can provide these same benefits. Playing bingo, for example, is good for people regardless of whether the bingo game takes place in the church basement or in a nonreligious community center. And there are many community organizations dedicated to pursuing work of great moral value that don't have religious connotations. Whether religious or not, people ought to look for a reason to get out of the house and interact with other people in socially beneficial ways.

Nonreligious people can even benefit from the lessons of prayer. Although atheists cannot pray to God, they can still set time aside for daily meditation. It is likely (although not scientifically proven to my knowledge) that many of the benefits of prayer are shared by nonreligious forms of meditation. I say this in no way to dismiss the personal relevance or metaphysical value of prayer. Instead, I merely want to emphasize that prayer and meditation, emotionally speaking, have a lot in common.

From my reading of the scientific literature, I believe that religious experiences make it easier for people to find happiness and help people to summon their emotional resilience. Religious people are more likely to believe the world is just than are nonreligious people, and such beliefs make it easier for people to overcome adversity. In communities with dominant religious organizations, people who belong to such organizations have emotional advantages over those who do not.

I certainly believe that Jay Schreiner's religious beliefs and practices are sincerely held. As he has struggled emotionally with the pain and disability brought on by his cancer, Jay has found much joy and peace of mind in his Roman Catholic faith. Cancer did not make Jay into a religious man, but it certainly focused more of his mental energy on the role that faith plays in his life. On the other hand, Andy Crawford's experience, as described in Chapter 9, shows the heights to which nonreligious people can aspire, even in times of adversity. Morality and selflessness are not the sole purview of religious people. Meaning and purpose are not the exclusive property of the faithful.

Jay Schreiner and Andy Crawford teach us that, in times of adversity, it is important to look inward and discover what is most important in your life, whether it be your spouse, your God, or your desire to change the world. And what a world it would be if more people, religious or nonreligious, could focus their energy so effectively.

When confronting adversity, many people find emotional resilience through their religious beliefs. Whether religion is right or wrong for any person, however, is a matter for each of us to decide.

Thinking Your Way to Happiness: It's All a Matter of Interpretation

One day, when I lived in Philadelphia, I got a ride to work from my friend Mike. Traffic was heavy and an obnoxious motorist was tailgating us on a dangerous highway, lovingly nicknamed "The Sure Kill" by locals. The motorist honked at us and flashed his lights, trying to get Mike to edge up higher above the speed limit, but Mike wouldn't budge. Exasperated, the tailgater recklessly passed us off the shoulder of the road, swerving in front of our car as he reentered the lane and barely missing Mike's front bumper. I was livid, my blood pressure, no doubt, shooting up to dangerous levels, as I sputtered obscenities at the windshield. But just as I was about to roll down my window and deliver my obscenities more effectively, Mike, who was driving the car after all, intervened and raised his hand at the offending vehicle. Glancing at Mike and expecting to see his middle finger prominently displayed, I instead saw only a small grin on his face as he gave the motorist a pleasant "hello" wave. Mike drove on with the smirk lingering on his face and muttered something to me about how people are in way too much of a hurry. He not only refused to let the motorist get on his nerves but enjoyed the opportunity to fool the motorist (and me) by delivering such an incongruent gesture.

Perhaps Mike is genetically mellower than I am, or maybe he was raised by peacenik parents who taught him how to cope with aggression. But Mike taught me that day that when someone cuts me off in traffic, I don't need to spend the next fifteen minutes in a lather. Mike showed me that happiness is often a matter of interpretation.

I consider myself to be a happier than average person (as so many of us do!). I do not experience very many bad moods, and the ones I do experience are rarely deep or long lasting. And yet with his simple hand gesture, Mike had shown me an area of my life where I was allowing myself to get unnecessarily aggravated. By choosing a different interpretation of the situation, Mike had not only avoided aggravation but had succeeded in amusing himself.

In this book, I have explained that struggles don't overwhelm people as often as they would have predicted. Rather than defeat us, struggles can actually make us stronger. I have explained that the way people respond to struggles, indeed the way they respond to life more generally, is strongly influenced by their DNA. But I have also given hints about the influence people's thinking has on their emotional resilience. It's time for me to take this theme a bit further. After all, most of us hope to find happiness in our lives, especially in times of adversity. And since we can't change our genetic heritage, it's important that we search out other ways to achieve the kind of happiness we want to achieve, other methods for boosting our emotional resilience.

The Hazards of Positive Thinking

As an adolescent, I was often grumpy about my love life, convinced that girls would never find me attractive. My poor beleaguered parents responded the way many good parents respond, by pleading with me to think about all the good things in my life. At the time, my response to this kind of exhortation was to think of how happy I would be if my parents stopped telling me how happy I should be. In fact, that response was probably typical. We all know that the power of positive thinking can't hold a candle to adolescent angst.

But unbeknownst to them, my parents were doling out dangerous advice to me, regardless of my age, because it does not always help to count up all one's blessings.

Take a moment to think of two positive events that happened to you today. I just took some time to do that and came up with the following: I had a nice quiet morning at home writing part of this book and a nice talk with my boss about recruiting a new faculty member to my research program. Thinking about these two positive events puts me in a good mood, just as my parents would have predicted.

Now, take a longer moment to think about *twelve* good things that happened to you today. After all, if thinking about two good events makes you happy, thinking about twelve should make you even happier. Here's what happened when I tried to think about twelve good events. Hmmm . . . I could remember some funny things my boys did before I dropped them off at day care and the beautiful farmland I drove past on my way to work this afternoon. I could remember a handful of other good events. But after thinking of six or seven good events, I started slowing down. Pretty soon, I get into a funk, wondering why it was so hard to think of twelve good events. Maybe my life is not so idyllic after all.

My colleague Norbert Schwarz, a social psychologist at the University of Michigan, has shown that most people can quickly make a list of six or seven positive events in their daily life, but they have a harder time thinking of eleven or twelve events. In fact, they struggle so hard to think of these last few positive events that they begin to doubt their own happiness. Consequently, those people whom he has asked to think about two good events in their lives end up happier than the people he has asked to think about twelve. The benefits of positive thinking in this latter group are overwhelmed by the doubts created when they realize the finiteness of the good events in their lives. Schwarz's research demonstrates that positive thinking does not always lead to positive results. But the flip side of this coin holds true, too—negative thinking does not always lead to negative results. For example, when asked to generate a list of twelve bad things going on in their lives, many people struggle to complete the list and, due to their struggles, conclude that their lives are pretty good!

As Schwarz's insight shows, happiness does not depend only on whether people think positive or negative thoughts. It also depends on how they interpret these thoughts. Indeed, Schwarz's research suggests that if you want to get into a good mood, think about a couple good things that have happened to you recently—but don't try to think of a whole bunch of things. And when confronted with negative thoughts, it might be useful to remind yourself of how few negative events you have experienced lately.

But even more important, Schwarz's research shows that given the same circumstances, people have wide interpretive latitude. All of our lives are a mixture of good and bad events. In deciding how happy we are with our lives, this mixture gives latitude for most of us to convince ourselves that our lives are pretty good.

Before/After Thinking

Of course, when people confront new struggles, and especially when they face permanent adversity, it is not always easy for them to convince themselves that life is very good anymore. However, another study Schwarz did suggests a way out of this trap. Schwarz asked a group of college freshmen to think about a "*positive* event that happened two years ago, that is, before you came to the university." He asked a second group to think about a *"negative* event" that happened before they came to the university. If Mom and Dad really know best, and positive thinking makes people happy, then the first group of freshmen, who were asked to think of a positive event, should be happier than the second group. But in fact, the opposite occurred. Students who thought about positive events were *less happy* than those who thought about negative events.

This strange result seems to contradict what we have just learned. Based on Schwarz's previous study, students who thought about one positive event should be happier than those who thought about one negative event, given how easy it was for them to conjure the single event.

But a different phenomenon occurred in this study. The students who thought about one positive event were unhappy because their thoughts put them into a nostalgic mood, yearning for glory days from their past. When they thought about a good event that they experienced before coming to the university, they reminisced about their high school proms or about how much fun it was to be a big man on campus. Thinking about these wonderful high school events made them unhappy because they interpreted these events as being part of their past.

By contrast, if they were anything like me, students asked to think about a bad event from high school reminisced about being abandoned by their dates halfway through the prom (I wish I were making this up), about boring classes filled with rote memorization, or about petty high school social hierarchies that fail to recognize the true appeal of intellectual accomplishment (I *really* wish I was making this up!). Thinking about these aspects of high school life would make just about any freshman happy to be in college.

When these college students reminisced about high school, they thought about it as part of their past and no longer contributing to their current happiness. But high school does not have to be interpreted this way. Instead, it can be thought of as part of what makes us who we are today. In fact, Schwarz asked a separate group of college freshmen to think about good and bad events "that happened two years ago," without adding the qualifying statement "that is, before you came to the university," and found that students' moods responded to positive and negative thoughts exactly the way our parents would predict: college freshmen who reminisced about a good event from the past two years were happier than those who reminisced about a bad event. When not reminded that events from two years ago occurred before they came to the university, students interpreted the events as being part of their current lives, or at least as part of what made them into the people they were that day.

"That was then, this is now" thinking is most likely to occur when people ponder discrete phases of their lives: high school years and college years; single life and married life; life before kids and life after all hell broke loose . . . stuff like that. Such before/after thinking is especially relevant to people who confront serious adversity, who can easily separate their lives into preillness/postillness phases, or predivorce/postdivorce periods. A person might think: "Before my stroke I could walk, now I can't." If people in these situations reminisce about all the good things in their lives before they faced a specific struggle, they are likely to become unhappy. They'll be more bitter about what they have lost and not be able to appreciate the good fortune they have experienced.

But Schwarz's research shows a potential way to escape the hazards of before/after thinking. People with illness and disability, or any kind of adversity, should embrace positive events from earlier in their lives, rather than bemoan such events for being part of their previous lives. People who were great athletes before becoming disabled should not get distressed reminiscing about their past glory days but should carry around those achievements as part of their present personality.

If that doesn't work, try to remember some bad things that used to happen in a previous stage of your life. Or focus on good things happening in your current life that hadn't happened in a previous stage. Perhaps before experiencing adversity you did not take the time to smell the proverbial roses. Well, be sure to smell them now and remind yourself that the sweet odor didn't used to be part of your life.

As Long as You Are Thinking Positive, Do It with Feeling!

One morning, while my wife and my youngest son, Taylor, were upstairs sleeping, my three-year-old boy, Jordan, and I sat downstairs at the breakfast table eating cereal. Busy yammering about something or other, Jordan was talking so much that he had forgotten to eat his cereal, so I reminded him to take a couple bites before it got soggy. I walked over to the refrigerator to get myself a glass of orange juice, came back, and saw him poised with his spoon in front of his mouth, looking up at me expectantly. On the spoon was not a pile of soggy cereal but a pacifier (which he'd only recently given up). He was pretending that he was going to eat his pacifier. I spewed orange juice across the table as I cracked up at his wonderful joke.

Why did I find this so funny? Hmmm, well let me think. Jordan wanted to see my reaction. He thought I would be expecting to see cereal on his spoon and would therefore be surprised at seeing the pacifier. This type of twist on normal happenings is a common comedic technique. But how or why did Jordan arrive at this? Well, he might have been looking for a way to delay eating his cereal, or for a way to hold on to his pacifier a little longer, or . . . aaargh! I've just taken the fun out of this experience. I'm analyzing it so much I can no longer see the humor in it.

But the fact is, it cracked me up at the time. The look on Jordan's face was so devilish as he patiently waited for me to see him that I was tempted to give him a big hug. And his idea was so creative, such a stroke of comedic genius.

Positive thinking leads to greater happiness if we connect it to our emotions. Just now, when I thought about how Jordan's joke made me *feel*, I reexperienced that mood. In fact, I found myself laughing again as I was typing the previous paragraph. Whereas, when I actually tried to analyze Jordan's pacifier joke, it deflated my positive mood.

Analytic thinking typically dampens people's moods. Spend a little time analyzing why you love your romantic partner and you won't soon swoon. But spend some time thinking about how your partner makes you feel and you will probably feel much better.

I don't mean to suggest that people shouldn't analyze their circumstances. Sometimes we need to figure out what's happening in our lives, even if we dampen our good moods in the process. In fact, when we are in bad moods, such critical thinking could come in handy. When people analyze negative events, when they think about why such events made them unhappy, their unhappiness often diminishes.

This dampening may explain why people in bad moods often engage in heavy analytical thinking. If we put on our Vulcan ears for a while, the emotional pain will go away and we might even figure out how to keep the bad event from happening again.

As you can see, when thinking back on good experiences in your life it does not always pay to analyze your feelings. Instead, you should focus on reliving the feelings. But even more important, you should embrace these experiences as fully as possible while they are happening. You need not wait until the reminiscing stage to maximize the emotional impact of these events. In fact, when people respond expressively to positive events, they gain more happiness from those events.

The psychologist Christopher Langston conducted a study in which he gave college students pagers and had them fill out diaries whenever their pagers went off. He directed students to record their moods, any recent positive events they had experienced, and the way they reacted to those positive events. He found that students who responded expressively to the positive events, by rewarding themselves with a beer or celebrating with friends, received longer lasting happiness from the events than students who responded less expressively. And these expressive responses were not simply a marker of people's baseline moods; the benefit of these expressive responses persisted even after Langston adjusted the data to reflect students' baseline moods. In other words, it wasn't simply that happy students jumped for joy and therefore remained happy. The jumping itself often reinforced and regenerated their joy!

Most important of all, when you experience something good in your life, share your feelings with a friend. Sharing good events increases the strength and duration of your positive feelings. This no doubt explains the popularity of birthday parties, wedding celebrations, and graduation ceremonies. Positive events take on more meaning when shared with the people we love. But such events need not be limited to formal occasions like weddings and graduations. Comedy films are usually funnier when we watch them with friends. We share the laughter and that leads to more laughter. Dancing is a good response to joy, but it is also a great way of creating joy. Positive moods can feed on themselves. And we can harness that phenomenon to our advantage. When we experience happy events in our lives, we should take time to savor these events and to celebrate them with friends. If we do so, they will bring us even greater happiness.

A "Think Your Way to Happiness" Primer

I am convinced happiness is often a matter of interpretation. But choosing the right way to interpret situations is not always easy. If you follow the logic of this chapter and hope to find happiness, then you will think about positive events that can be interpreted as part of your current life and you will do so with feeling. When plagued with negative events, you will think of them as part of your past life or, when that's not possible, analyze these events to dampen or even defuse your bad mood.

People struggling through adversity increase their happiness by making downward social comparisons, by utilizing counterfactual thinking, or by shifting their goals and expectations. And, if positive moods are hard to come by, they can convince themselves that moods are less important to their happiness than pursuing a life directed toward meaningful pursuits.

Indeed, as a result of the research I conducted in writing this book—the studies I conducted with my research collaborators, the patients I interviewed, and the readings I immersed myself in for each of the chapters—I have changed the way I practice medicine. I now find myself focusing on a number of ways to help my patients improve their lives, especially those patients who are struggling with major health problems.

Set Realistic Expectations

Medically speaking, of course, I try to maximize my patients' function, prescribing medicines for their heart failure or physical therapy for their back problems or whatever other interventions I think will improve their health. I teach them exercises to help them strengthen their bodies and overcome some of their health-related limitations. I encourage yoga or meditation or other interventions for people with chronic pain or anxiety. But all the while, I recognize that few people in their middle age, and even fewer in old age, will live a life free of physical limitations. And so a real key to overcoming the emotional impact of such limitations is to develop realistic expectations of their physical performance and functioning. Some people, despite the wonders of medical therapy, will experience pain every day of their lives. Joints wear out. Nerves get damaged. Eventually, people need to deal with their pain, or their shortness of breath, or whatever problems plague them. We can't cure everything, so we have to learn how to accept the things we can't change.

I have noticed that once they accept that it will never go away many patients actually feel as if their pain has diminished. Many patients tell me they are frustrated that their physical endurance is limited by joint problems, circulatory troubles, or other disease processes. I work with these patients to devise strategies for maximizing their function. But I also work with them to overcome their frustrations. I don't believe in being complacent in the face of adversity. But neither do I believe in banging your head against a brick wall. Studies of elderly people confirm, in fact, that successful aging is not merely a function of remaining healthy and fit as long as possible, but also depends in significant part on adjusting expectation to fit reality. Imagine what Scott Mackler's life would be like if he still yearned to run marathons.

Strive for Intrinsically Meaningful Goals

At the same time that I work with my patients to make sure that they have realistic expectations, I also try to find out what goals they have in their lives. My main purpose is to do what I can to make sure they have something in their lives that they are striving to achieve. I don't bother to get "existential" with my patients. I don't judge the social or moral value of their goals. Instead, I believe that it is important for their mental health and emotional resilience to choose goals that they care about, regardless of whether I would choose to pursue similar goals.

I read in a magazine once about an elderly man whose goal in life was to read the *New York Times* every day from cover to cover. With the exception of things like advertisements and stock market figures, he was determined to read every word of every story every day. He was so determined, in fact, that he didn't allow himself to become bothered when his reading pace slowed down, and he started to fall behind. He could no longer make it through all seven newspapers each week, so he collected the papers and kept reading them in the order they arrived. Eventually he fell years behind in his reading. To keep the goal fresh, however, he refused to look at any other news source, preferring to fall behind in his knowledge of world events than to interrupt the joy he received from reading each day's *New York Times*. For all I know, he's trying to figure out right now whether Iraq has weapons of mass destruction. Motivated by his goal of reading the newspaper, he gets out of bed each day determined to read as much as possible and excited to find out what has gone on in the world.

I mention this man because his goals are clearly absurd. Yet he is still better off, in my opinion, than people who lack a driving force like this in their lives. His story is certainly peculiar. How many people would refuse to keep up with the news in order to pursue such a strange obsession? But is it any more absurd than spending thousands of hours practicing chip shots on a golf course, or completing crossword puzzles, or planting flowers in your garden? We all need to think about what gives our lives meaning and purpose. And we need to decide how much of our time to spend on selfish pursuits (like my daily piano practicing) versus more socially valuable pursuits.

We must decide. More important, we need to decide to decide. The unexamined life very well may be worth living, but it is rarely as worthwhile as the examined life.

One morning, a patient walked into my clinic and told me, "Doc, I didn't get out of my pajamas yesterday." I pushed aside any concerns I had had about his mildly elevated blood pressure and spent my time with him finding out how he spent most of his days. He was unemployed and his mother, whose home he still lived in, had died eighteen months ago. Since that time, he had had little motivation to get out of the house. His situation was extreme and complicated by depression, which I co-treated with a psychiatrist. But he was also suffering from a less extreme problem. He was suffering from a paucity of goals. He wasn't striving for anything anymore.

We all need a reason to get out of our pajamas every morning. I counsel some of my patients, those I see struggling with their illnesses or disabilities, to set aside fifteen minutes each day to write down their goals. I tell them they can write about what their goals are for the next day or for the next year or for the remainder of their lives. When possible, I set aside time on follow-up clinic visits to see what progress they have made. I've been surprised on some follow-up visits to find out how well my advice has worked. Several of my patients have told me that in response to this exercise they began to perform volunteer work. These patients had been unable to hold down full-time jobs because of their health problems, but they had found volunteer positions that were more flexible, where they could show up on good days and stay home on bad days. These patients now had good reason to get out of their pajamas.

Don't Wait for Adversity

None of us should need to wait for significant challenges to come our way in order to focus our lives on pursuits that we care about. But nevertheless we often fall into this trap. And this trap is nothing new. Almost a century ago, a magazine asked the writer Marcel Proust to imagine that the world was about to end. It asked him to predict how people would respond, probably expecting him to spin a wild tale of desperation or debauchery. But instead, Proust responded:

> I think that life would suddenly seem wonderful to us if we were threatened to die. Just think of how many projects, travels, love affairs, studies, it—our life—hides from us, made invisible by our laziness which, certainty of a future, delays

incessantly. But let all this threaten to become impossible forever, how beautiful it would become again!

The cataclysm doesn't happen, we don't do any of it, because we find ourselves back in the heart of normal life, where negligence deadens desire. And yet we shouldn't have needed the cataclysm to live life today. It should've been enough to think that we are humans, and that death may come this evening.

Emotional resilience lies within all of us, waiting to be called upon when we face difficult struggles. But we need not wait for adversity to summon the powers that contribute to our resilience. Resilience lies within our DNA, and we can call upon it at any time we like. The world is stacked with meaningful goals to pursue, from spending quality time with friends and family to starting health care clinics in Bangladesh. We can all summon the discipline to reflect on our lives and pursue the goals we care about the most.

Epilogue

It was the first day of kindergarten for my youngest boy, Taylor, but I was the one who was nervous. Not about kindergarten. I knew Taylor would soon be regaling us with tales about his new best friends. Instead, I was nervous about Greg and Ruth Hughes, about their reaction to what I was planning to write about them in my book. I had mailed some chapter drafts to them several weeks earlier and was driving to their house to get their feedback. I was anxious about whether I had made a bunch of mistakes in describing their lives, or whether anything I wrote would offend them. I arrived at their house and prepared myself for their line-by-line critique.

As it turned out, we didn't get much opportunity to go over the chapters that day because the chapters were circulating among family members and Greg and Ruth hadn't had a chance to retrieve them yet. My writings had been a major source of amusement for the Hughes family for the past three weeks, with people reveling in details about Greg's life. Almost no one missed an opportunity to make fun of Greg for being "on the record" for refusing to do housework, a little tidbit that struck a chord among all the women in the Hughes family.

But it wasn't the little details about Greg's life that generated most of the family discussion. Instead, people had begun talking to each other more about what it would be like to lose their legs. They began rethinking Greg's life. And after seeing what I had written about emotional resilience and about Greg's way of dealing with his circumstances, they had reached a general consensus—most felt that they would rather be dead than be in Greg's situation. Ruth teared up a bit as she told me this conclusion, admitting that she, too, had come to this same conclusion. Greg sat on the other side of the room petting a cat and looking unperturbed.

"It's not as bad as all that," he said.

"But honey," she replied, "you've had so much taken away."

"But you get it back," Greg answered. "You find other things."

"*You* find other things, Greg. I couldn't. I'd just get bitter."

It had been a few years now since Greg's amputations, and he had had many things taken away. He'd also experienced a series of new health problems. Since his amputations, he had gained lots of weight and as a result he developed diabetes. His kidneys were beginning to fail, partly as a result of his diabetes but mostly because of damage that occurred during the time of his initial hospitalization when he was in an intensive care unit and his blood pressure was fluctuating wildly. Greg's heart was having a difficult time, too. He had had nine balloon angioplasty procedures over the past two years to open up his coronary arteries, in hopes of preventing a heart attack.

Although Greg's life had not been easy since his amputations, he relished the good parts of his life, the parts he had "gotten back." He proudly told me he was driving again, having installed a device in his truck that allowed him to control braking and accelerating with his left hand. He had recently had cataract surgery, too, and was excited about how clear and colorful everything looked again. That's why Greg couldn't accept Ruth's conclusion about his life. He knew the powers of emotional resilience firsthand. He knew the alternative to resilience, too, and saw no reason why Ruth, in similar circumstances, would fare any worse. "Why would you be bitter?" he asked. "It's not like it would be anyone's fault if you lost your legs." In essence, Greg told Ruth that she is stronger than she thinks.

On my way home from Greg and Ruth's house that day, I dropped by Sarah Lezotte's home. She was now three years removed from her kidney transplant and had remained in good health. Having read the chapter draft I had sent her, however, she was struggling with the whole idea of emotional resilience. The chapter prompted her to think back on her life when she was receiving dialysis, and she wasn't ready to call that period of her life a happy time. "I wasn't truly happy then," she said. "Maybe content. I had had to give so much up during that time, and I'm so happy to have those parts of my life back again." She didn't question her previous emotional resilience. But she wondered how she could have maintained such a positive attitude throughout all her medical struggles. She's not sure she could ever find such strength again.

In thinking back on her dialysis days, she compared it to visiting her childhood home: "You remember your home being so big but when you see it again, you realize how small it was." Reminiscing on her dialysis life from her new perspective, she now recognizes how bad it was.

I could relate to Sarah's before/after change in perspective, albeit on a much smaller scale, having experienced a temporary disability more than a decade ago. It happened during my first year as a faculty member at the University of Pennsylvania when I had spent so much time writing research grants that I developed repetitive strain injury in my hands. I was unable to type at a computer because of pain so bad that I had difficulty holding a newspaper or driving a car or playing piano. For six months, I wore wrist splints and stayed away from pianos and computers.

In the first month or so, I was busy trying to make sure I could still keep writing grants at work, trying to sleep at night despite the pain, and trying to figure out what was causing this trouble. But soon I started sleeping better (thanks to the splints) and I was able to adapt to my situation. I didn't play piano anymore, but I listened to lots of music, more music than I had had time to listen to in a long while. I didn't type at a computer, but I wrote papers by speaking into a tape recorder, a practice I maintain to this day. I found ways to do everyday tasks with as little use of my hands as possible.

Eventually my hands improved. After six months of staying away from the piano, six months of abandoning a hobby that had consumed me since age five, I was able to start playing piano again and now, ten years later, I can play as much piano as I like.

My life is clearly better now than it was then. Yet if I had carried around a PDA during my six month hiatus from piano playing and recorded my moment-to-moment moods, I expect that I would have been just as happy then as I am today, in the same way that Sarah reported being happy when she was on dialysis. But looking back on that time, I can see the void. I had replaced piano playing with other worthwhile and challenging pursuits, but life hadn't been the same. From my current vantage point, my life during those six months seems so much more limited, the way Sarah's childhood home has shrunk over the years. Sarah's retrospective view of her life on dialysis illustrates the great paradox of emotional resilience. She experienced truly horrendous circumstances and responded with great emotional strength, retaining most of the optimism and positive energy that had characterized her personality before she became ill. She had the strength to find happiness, or contentedness, despite her ordeal. Having lived with a successful transplant now for three years, her life is better by any objective measure. But don't expect this to be reflected much in her moment-to-moment moods. Emotions tend to stabilize over time. Sarah hasn't walked around in a perpetual state of glee for three years.

Instead, many of the things that made her happy when she was sick are making her happy now. When I visited her to discuss the book chapter, she was several days removed from her seventy-second birthday. She was excited to tell me about the surprise birthday party her family had thrown, attended by more than eighty people. In fact, as we visited that day, she kept finding ways of directing our conversation to one or another of her children or grandchildren. She currently had fourteen grandchildren and was very happy to announce that a fifteenth grandchild was soon on the way.

The greatest joy in Sarah's life comes from spending time with family. And her health problems never took away that source of joy.

Not long after returning from Sarah's house, I received a call from Jay Schreiner, whom I had also asked to look over some book chapters. Even though his chordoma had continued to progress, Jay was as optimistic as ever. He had lost most of the use of one hand now, and the skin on the back of his neck had become so thin from his previous surgeries that Jay's doctors were considering placing a skin graft there, a procedure they planned to perform in a few months at the same time they removed a tumor that was growing out from the front of Jay's neck. Jay's life continues in a cycle of surgical intervention and recovery, and Jay remains as undaunted as ever. He continues to spend a lot of time with M.B. and is undergoing experimental chemotherapy with the hope that this will halt or slow down his tumor.

I spoke with M.B. that same day, and she had a few concerns about my writing. In particular, she wanted to make sure that people didn't make too much of the age difference between her and Jay: "I don't want people thinking Jay ran off and married some young babe," she told me. I heard Jay yelling in the background: "But I did run off and marry a young babe!"

Jay's mischievous reply aside, I understood M.B.'s point completely. In fact, in the time I've had the pleasure of spending with Jay and M.B., I've never felt like I was with an older man and a younger woman. Instead, I feel as if I'm with a marvelously matched couple. Jay's energy level and enthusiasm, the mischievous twinkle in his eyes—these are all traits that make him come off as being much younger than he is. If anything, M.B. comes off as the stable, mature member of the household.

Scott Mackler remains a source of stability in his household, too. His oldest son, Alexander, who was sixteen years old when his dad developed amyotrophic lateral sclerosis (ALS), has now graduated from college and is working for Emily's List. His younger brother, Noah, is still in school, visiting his dad in his research lab whenever he can.

Scott is increasingly traveling around the country to lecture at medical schools. He paid a visit to Michigan not long ago and gave a standing-room-only lecture to medical students describing his experience with ALS. After the talk, Scott had about an hour to recuperate before heading over to a research building to lecture a group of addiction researchers about his latest scientific findings. These dueling talks are indicative of Scott's life. His life is not about ALS. He's not about to write an inspirational memoir about his struggle with the disease. That would take away from the time he has to devote to his scientific work. ALS is obviously a huge part of Scott's life, but it is not his *raison d'être*. ALS is an obstacle, but one that he continues to struggle against in order to accomplish the things that matter in his life.

Scott doesn't know if his research will lead to a cure for cocaine addiction. But he continues to plug away at the problem in hopes of making the world a better place. Cocaine addiction is not a simple problem that will go away anytime soon. His ambitious pursuit is somewhat reminiscent of Andy Crawford's Bangladesh efforts. Like Andy, Scott chose to pursue a goal that is likely to elude him. And like Andy, Scott recognizes that the pursuit of such goals is worthy in its own right. What's more, the pursuit of ambitious goals often leads to worthwhile intermediate achievements—Andy changed many people's lives with his passion. Scott continues to uncover mysteries of the molecular underpinnings of mammalian life. Who knows where the knowledge he has created will lead?

Scott's influence won't cease when he dies, whether his death happens one year or forty years from now. Science is a community enterprise and, as a scientist, Scott has laid the groundwork for other scientists to build upon. In this way, too, Scott is a lot like Andy

Crawford. Andy died before he could open a clinic in Bangladesh, but he had laid the groundwork for his son to complete the work. Determined to follow through on his dad's dream, Alex continued to chip away at the many layers of resistance he encountered in Bangladesh. And within several years of his dad's death, he accomplished even more than his father had originally envisioned, bringing health care to thousands of people who would otherwise have gone without such care.

Most of us don't have the skills or the gumption to develop a cure for cocaine addiction or to start up a series of health care clinics in Bangladesh. But most of us do have a wellspring of emotional resilience to draw upon in time of need. And with such resilience, we can make our lives—and the lives of people around us—better.

I was reminded of the subtle but important ways people improve the world during one of my trips to Greg and Ruth's house. As we sat around talking, the two of them somehow got on the topic of practical jokes. One joke in particular amused them, as they reminisced about a time when Greg had gotten his hands on a mask of an old man, a truly frightening visage that he had donned on more than one occasion to amuse his friends. One night, he put the mask on and laid down in bed, waiting for Ruth to enter the bedroom. When she did, she was so frightened at seeing the old man lying in their bed, she went into a panic attack and Greg had to call 911. She survived the ordeal, of course, and now practically becomes apoplectic with laughter when joining in on the retelling of the story.

I carry no illusions of discovering a cure for cocaine addiction in my lifetime or of transforming the health system of a Third World country. But I hope to change the world in small but important ways, much the way Greg's sense of humor enriches the lives of the people lucky enough to spend time with him.

Greg has changed a great deal over the past few years. He is more philosophical than he used to be. And more laidback. But more sur-

prising than all of this, Greg has undergone another kind of trans-
formation. Greg has started helping out with housework. Never in
his life could he have imagined such a fate. And never would he have
predicted that he'd not only help out with the housework, but that
he wouldn't even be bothered by doing such work. Even Greg, it
seems, underestimated his own strength.

References

Chapter 1: The Beginning of the Struggle

Brickman, P., D. Coates, and R. Janoff-Bulman. "Lottery Winners and Accident Victims: Is Happiness Relative?" *Journal of Personality & Social Psychology* 36, no. 8 (1978): 917–27.

di Tella, R., and R. MacCulloch. "The Macroeconomics of Happiness." *Review of Economics and Statistics* 85 (2003): 809–27.

Frederick, S., and G. Loewenstein. "Hedonic Adaptation." In *Well-Being: The Foundations of Hedonic Psychology*, edited by D. Kahneman, E. Diener, and N. Schwarz. New York: Russell Sage Foundation Press, 1999.

Pavot, W., E. Diener, C. R. Colvin, et al. "Further Validation of the Satisfaction with Life Scale: Evidence for the Cross-Method Convergence of Well-Being Measures." *Journal of Personality Assessment* 57 (1991): 149–61.

Sandvik, E., E. Diener, and L. Seidlitz. "Subjective Well-Being: The Convergence and Stability of Self-Report and Non-Self-Report Measures." *Journal of Personality* 61, no. 3 (1993): 317–42.

Schwarz, N., and G. L. Clore. "Mood, Misattribution, and Judgments of Well-Being: Informative and Directive Functions of Affective States." *Journal of Personality & Social Psychology* 45, no. 3 (1983): 513–23.

Schwarz, N., and F. Strack. "Evaluating One's Life: A Judgment Model of Subjective Well-Being. In *Subjective Well-Being 1st ed.*, edited by F. Strack, M. Argyle, and N. Schwarz, 27–47. Oxford: Pergamon Press, 1991.

Chapter 2: The Limits of the Imagination

Boyd, N. F., H. J. Sutherland, K. Z. Heasman, et al. "Whose Utilities for Decision Analysis?" *Medical Decision Making* 10, no. 1 (1990): 58–67.

Fredrickson, B. L., and D. Kahneman. "Duration Neglect in Retrospective Evaluations of Affective Episodes." *Journal of Personality & Social Psychology* 65, no. 1 (1993): 45–55.

Gilbert, D. T., E. C. Pinel, and T. D. Wilson. "Immune Neglect: A Source of Durability Bias in Affective Forecasting." *Journal of Personality & Social Psychology* 75, no. 3 (1998): 617–38.

Kahneman, D., B. L. Fredrickson, C. A. Schreiber, et al. "When More Pain Is Preferred to Less: Adding a Better End." *Psychological Science* 4, no. 6 (1993): 401–5.

Keller, M. C., B. L. Fredrickson, O. Ybarra, et al. "A Warm Heart and a Clear Head: The Contingent Effects of Weather on Mood and Cognition." *Psychological Science* 16, no. 9 (Sept. 2005): 724–31.

Read, D., and G. Loewenstein. "Diversification Bias: Explaining the Discrepancy in Variety Seeking Between Combined and Separated Choices." *Journal of Experimental Psychology:Applied* 1 (1995): 34–49.

Redelmeier, D. A., and D. Kahneman. "Patient's Memories of Painful Medical Treatments: Real-Time and Retrospective Evaluations of Two Minimally Invasive Procedures." *Pain* 116 (1996): 3–8.

Riis, J., G. Loewenstein, J. Baron, et al. "Ignorance of Hedonic Adaptation to Hemo-Dialysis: A Study Using Ecological Momentary Assessment." *Journal of Experimental Psychology: General* 134, no. 1 (2005): 3–9.

Schkade, D. A., and D. Kahneman. "Does Living in California Make People Happy? A Focusing Illusion in Judgments of Life Satisfaction." *Psychological Science* 9 (1998): 340–46.

Smith, D. M., R.L. Sherriff, G. Loewenstein, et al. "Misremembering Colostomies? Former Patients Give Lower Utility Ratings Than Do Current Patients." *Health Psychology* (In Press).

Ubel, P. A., G. Loewenstein, J. Hershey, et al. "Do Nonpatients Underestimate the Quality of Life Associated with Chronic Health Conditions Because of a Focusing Illusion?" *Medical Decision Making* 21, no. 3 (2001): 190–99.

Ubel, P. A., G. Loewenstein, C. Jepson, et al. "Disability and Sunshine: Can Predictions Be Improved by Drawing Attention to Focusing Illusions or Emotional Adaptation?" *Journal of Experimental Psychology:Applied* 11, no. 2 (2005):111–23.

Wilson, T. D., T. Wheatley, J. M. Meyers, et al. "Focalism: A Source of Durability Bias in Affective Forecasting." *Journal of Personality & Social Psychology* 78, no. 5 (2000): 821–36.

Chapter 3: Happiness: Circumstance or DNA?

Carver, C. S., C. Pozo, S. D. Harris, et al. "How Coping Mediates the Effect of Optimism on Distress: A Study of Women with Early Stage Breast Cancer." *Journal of Personality & Social Psychology* 65, no. 2 (Aug. 1993): 375–90.

Costa, P. T., Jr., R. R. McCrae, and A. B. Zonderman. "Environmental and Dispositional Influences on Well-Being: Longitudinal Follow-Up of an American National Sample." *British Journal of Psychology* 78 (1987): 299–306.

DeNeve, K. M., and H. Cooper. "The Happy Personality: A Meta-Analysis of 137 Personality Traits and Subjective Well-Being." *Psychological Bulletin* 124, no. 2 (1998): 197–229.

Ditto, P. H., and J. B. I. Jemmott. "From Rarity to Evaluative Extremity: Effects of Prevalence Information on Evaluations of Positive and Negative Characteristics." *Journal of Personality & Social Psychology* 57 (1989): 16–26.

Eronen, S., and J. Nurmi. "Life Events, Predisposing Cognitive Strategies and Well-Being." *European Journal of Personality* 13 (1999): 129–48.

Goldberg, L. R. "The Development of Markers for the Big-Five Factor Structure." *Psychological Assessment* 4, no. 1 (1992): 26–42.

Headey, B., and A. Wearing. "Personality, Life Events, and Subjective Well-Being: Toward a Dynamic Equilibrium Model." *Journal of Personality & Social Psychology* 57, no. 4 (1989): 731–39.

Lyubomirsky, S. "Why Are Some People Happier Than Others? The Role of Cognitive and Motivational Processes in Well-Being." *American Psychologist* 56, no. 3 (2001): 239–49.

Lyubomirsky, S., and L. Ross. "Changes in Attractiveness of Elected, Rejected, and Precluded Alternatives: A Comparison of Happy and Unhappy Individuals." *Journal of Personality & Social Psychology* 76, no. 6 (1999): 988–1007.

Nagel, T. "What Is It Like to Be a Bat?" In *The Mind's I: Fantasies and Reflections on Self and Soul*, edited by D. R. Hofstadter and D. C. Dennett, 391–402. New York: Bantam Books, 1981.

Scheier, M. F., K. A. Matthews, J. F. Owens, et al. "Dispositional Optimism and Recovery from Coronary Artery Bypass Surgery: The Beneficial Effects on Physical and Psychological Well-Being." *Journal of Personality & Social Psychology* 57, no. 6 (1989): 1024–40.

Steel, P., and D. S. Ones. "Personality and Happiness: A National-Level Analysis." *Journal of Personality & Social Psychology* 83, no. 3 (2002): 767–81.

Suh, E., E. Diener, and F. Fujita. "Events and Subjective Well-Being: Only Recent Events Matter." *Journal of Personality & Social Psychology* 70, no. 5 (1996): 1091–102.

Tellegen, A., D. T. Lykken, T. J. Bouchard, Jr., et al. "Personality Similarity in Twins Reared Apart and Together." *Journal of Personality & Social Psychology* 54, no. 6 (1988): 1031–39.

Chapter 4: Responding to Adversity

Affleck, G., and H. Tennen. "Construing Benefits from Adversity: Adaptational Significance and Dispositional Underpinnings." *Journal of Personality* 64, no. 4 (1996): 899–922.

Albrecht, G. L., and P. J. Devlieger. "The Disability Paradox: High Quality of Life Against All Odds." *Social Science and Medicine* 48, no. 8 (Feb. 15, 1999): 977–88.

Brown, J. D., and K. A. Dutton. "Truth and Consequences: The Costs and Benefits of Accurate Self-Knowledge." *Personality and Social Psychology* Bulletin 21, no. 12 (1995): 1288–96.

Bulman, R. J., and C. B. Wortman. "Attributions of Blame and Coping in the 'Real World': Severe Accident Victims React to Their Lot." *Journal of Personality & Social Psychology* 35, no. 5 (1977): 351–63.

Cash, T. F. C., D. Walker, and J. W. Butters. "Mirror, Mirror, on the Wall . . . ?: Contrast Effects and Self-Evaluations of Physical Attractiveness." *Personality and Social Psychology* Bulletin 9, no. 3 (1983): 351–58.

Christakis, D. A. *Death Foretold: Prophecy and Prognosis in Medical Care.* Chicago: University of Chicago Press, 2001.

Collins, R. L., S. E. Taylor, and L. A. Skokan. "A Better World or Shattered Vision? Changes in Life Perspectives Following Victimization." *Social Cognition* 8, no. 3 (1990): 263–85.

Danner, D. D., D. A. Snowdon, and W. V. Friesen. "Positive Emotions in Early Life and Longevity: Findings from the Nun Study." *Journal of Personality & Social Psychology* 80, no. 5 (May 2001): 804–13.

Decker, S. D., and R. Schulz. "Correlates of Life Satisfaction and Depression in Middle-Aged and Elderly Spinal Cord-Injured Persons." *American Journal of Occupational Therapy* 39, no. 11 (1985): 740–45.

Folkman, S. "Positive Psychological States and Coping with Severe Stress." *Social Science & Medicine* 45, no. 8 (1997): 1207–21.

Fredrickson, B. L. "The Role of Positive Emotions in Positive Psychology: The Broaden-and-Build Theory of Positive Emotions." *American Psychologist* 56, no. 3 (Mar. 2001): 218–26.

Friedman, M., and R. H. Rosenman. *Type A Behavior and Your Heart*: New York: Fawcett, 1982.

Helgeson, V. S., and S. E. Taylor. "Social Comparisons and Adjustment Among Cardiac Patients." *Journal of Applied Social Psychology* 23, no. 15 (1993): 1171–95.

Isen, A. M. "Positive Affect and Decision Making." In *Handbook of Emotions, 2nd ed.*, edited by M. Lewis and J. M. Haviland-Jones, 417–35. New York: The Guilford Press, 2000.

Kahneman, D. "Varieties of Counterfactual Thinking." In *What Might Have Been: The Social Psychology of Counterfactual Thinking*, edited by N. J. Roese and J. M. Olson, 375–96. Mahwah, NJ: Lawrence Erlbaum Associates, 1995.

Lehman, D. R., C. Wortman, S. Bluck, et al. "Positive and Negative Life Changes Following Bereavement and Their Relations to Adjustment." *Journal of Social and Clinical Psychology* 12, no. 1 (1993): 90–112.

McKenna, F. P., and I. P. Albery. "Does Unrealistic Optimism Change Following a Negative Experience?" *Journal of Applied Social Psychology* 31, no. 6 (2001): 1146–57.

Medvec, V. H., S. F. Madey, and T. Gilovich. "When Less Is More: Counterfactual Thinking and Satisfaction Among Olympic Medalists." *Journal of Personality & Social Psychology* 69, no. 4 (1995): 603–10.

Miller, G. E., A. K. Ritchey, and S. Cohen. "Chronic Psychological Stress and the Regulation of Pro-Inflammatory Cytokines: A Glucocorticoid-Resistance Model." *Health Psychology* 21, no. 6 (2002): 531–41.

Pike, C. "Nursing Care Study: The 'Broken Heart Syndrome' and the Elderly Patient." *Nursing Times* 79, no. 9 (Mar. 2–8, 1983): 50–53.

Price, R. *A Whole New Life: An Illness and a Healing.* New York: Antheneum, 1994.

Pyszczynski, T., J. Greenberg, and J. La Prelle. "Social Comparison After Success and Failure: Biased Search for Information Consistent with a Self-Serving Conclusion." *Journal of Experimental Social Psychology* 21 (1985): 195–211.

Roese, N. J. "Counterfactual Thinking." *Psychological Bulletin* 121, no. 1 (1997): 133–48.

Sapolsky, R. M. *Why Zebras Don't Get Ulcers, 3rd ed.* New York: Henry Holt and Company, LLC, 2004.

Taylor, S. E. "Asymmetrical Effects of Positive and Negative Events: The Mobilization-Minimization Hypothesis." *Psychological Bulletin* 110, no. 1 (1991): 67–85.

Taylor, S.E. *Positive Illusions, Creative Self-Deception and the Healthy Mind.* New York: Basic Books, Inc., 1989.

Taylor, S. E., and D. A. Armor. "Positive Illusions and Coping with Adversity." *Journal of Personality* 64, no. 4 (1996): 873–98.

Taylor, S. E., V. S. Helgeson, G. M. Reed, et al. "Self-Generated Feelings of Control and Adjustment to Physical Illness." *Journal of Social Issues* 47, no. 4 (1991): 91–109.

Taylor, S. E., M. E. Kemeny, G. M. Reed, et al. "Assault on the Self: Positive Illusions and Adjustment to Threatening Events." In *The Self: Interdisciplinary Approaches*, edited by J. S. G. R. Goethals, 239–54. New York: Springer-Verlag, 1991.

Taylor, S. E., and M. Lobel. "Social Comparison Activity Under Threat: Downward Evaluation and Upward Contacts." *Psychological Review* 96, no. 4 (1989): 569–75.

Wittstein, I. S., D. R. Thiemann, J. A. C. Lima, et al. "Neurohumoral Features of Myocardial Stunning Due to Sudden Emotional Stress." *New England Journal of Medicine* 352 (Feb. 2005): 539–48.

Wood, J. V., S. E. Taylor, and R. R. Lichtman. "Social Comparison in Adjustment to Breast Cancer." *Journal of Personality & Social Psychology* 49, no. 5 (1985): 1169–83.

Chapter 5: Uncertain Resilience

Ellsberg, D. "Risk, Ambiguity, and the Savage Axioms." *Quarterly Journal of Economics* 75 (1961): 643–69.

Frederick, S., and G. Loewenstein. "Hedonic Adaptation." In *Well-Being: The Foundations of Hedonic Psychology*, edited by D. Kahneman, E. Diener, and N. Schwarz. New York: Russell Sage Foundation Press, 1999.

Gerhart, K. A., R. L. Johnson, and G. G. Whiteneck. "Health and Psychosocial Issues of Individuals with Incomplete and Resolving Spinal Cord Injuries." *Paraplegia* 30 (1992): 282–87.

Hartkopp, A., H. Bronnum-Hansen, A. M. Seidenschnur, et al. "Suicide in a Spinal Cord Injured Population: Its Relation to Functional Status." *The Archives of Physical Medicine and Rehabilitation* 79 (1998): 1356–61.

Kubler-Ross, E. *On Death and Dying*. New York: Simon & Schuster, 1969.

Perry, S., L. Jacobsberg, and B. Fishman. "Suicidal Ideation and HIV Testing." *Journal of the American Medical Association* 263, no. 5 (1990): 679–82.

Sapolsky, R. M. *Why Zebras Don't Get Ulcers, 3rd ed.* New York: Henry Holt and Company, LLC, 2004.

Wiggins, S., P. Whyte, M. Huggins, et al. "The Psychological Consequences of Predictive Testing for Huntington's Disease. Canadian Collaborative Study of Predictive Testing." *New England Journal of Medicine* 327, no. 20 (1992): 1401–5.

Chapter 6: The Social Side of Adversity

Axelrod, R., and W. D. Hamilton. "The Evolution of Cooperation." *Science* 211, no. 27 (Mar. 1981): 1390–96.

Baumeister, R. F., and M. R. Leary. "The Need to Belong: Desire for Interpersonal Attachments as a Fundamental Human Motivation." *Psychology Bulletin* 117 (1995): 497–529.

Brown, S. L., R. M. Nesse, A. D. Vionkur, et al. "Providing Social Support May Be More Beneficial Than Receiving It: Results from a Prospective Study of Mortality." *Psychological Science* 14, no. 4 (2003): 320–27.

Case, R. B., A. J. Moss, N. Case, et al. "Living Alone After Myocardial Infarction. Impact on Prognosis." *Journal of the American Medical Association* 267, no. 4 (1992): 515–19.

Goodwin, P. J., M. Leszcz, M. Ennis, et al. "The Effect of Group Psychosocial Support on Survival in Metastatic Breast Cancer." *New England Journal of Medicine* 345, no. 24 (Dec. 13, 2001): 1719–26.

House, J. S., K. R. Landis, and D. Umberson. "Social Relationships and Health." In *The Society and Population Health Reader*, edited by I. Kawachi, B. P. Kennedy, and R. G. Wilkinson, 161–70. New York: The New Press, 1999.

Lander, D. L., and L. Montgomery. *Falling Down, Laughing: How Squiggy Caught Multiple Sclerosis and Didn't Tell Nobody*. New York: Jeremy P. Tarcher/Putnam, 2000.

Rabin, R. *Six Parts Love: A Family's Battle with Lou Gehrig's Disease (ALS)*. New York: Charles Scriber's Sons, 1985.

Rollins, B. C., and K. L. Cannon. "Marital Satisfaction over the Family Life Cycle: A Re-Evaluation." *Journal of Marriage and the Family* (1974): 271–82.

Sapolsky, R.M. *Why Zebras Don't Get Ulcers, 3rd ed*. New York: Henry Holt and Company, LLC, 2004.

Williams, R. B., J. C. Barefoot, R. M. Califf, et al. "Prognostic Importance of Social and Economic Resources Among Medically Treated Patients with Angiographically Documented Coronary Artery Disease." *Journal of the American Medical Association* 267, no. 4 (1992): 520–24.

Chapter 7: The Struggle to Overcome Small Nuisances

Csikszentmihalyi, M. *Flow: The Psychology of Optimal Experience.* New York: Harper and Row Publishers Inc., 1990.

Loewenstein, G. "Hedonic Adaptation." In *Well-Being: The Foundations of Hedonic Psychology,* edited by D. Kahneman, E. Diener, and N. Schwarz. New York: Russell Sage Foundation Press, 1999.

Mehnert, T., H. H. Krauss, R. Nadler, et al. "Correlates of Life Satisfaction in Those with Disabling Conditions." *Rehabilitation Psychology* 35, no. 1 (1990): 3–17.

Weinstein, N. D. "Community Noise Problems: Evidence Against Adaptation." *Journal of Environmental Psychology* 2 (1982): 87–97.

Chapter 8: Money Matters

Brickman, P., D. Coates, and R. Janoff-Bulman. "Lottery Winners and Accident Victims: Is Happiness Relative?" *Journal of Personality & Social Psychology* 36, no. 8 (1978): 917–27.

Clark, A. E., and A. J. Oswald. "Satisfaction and Comparison Income." *Journal of Public Economics* 61 (1996): 359–81.

Csikszentmihalyi, M. "If We Are So Rich, Why Aren't We Happy?" *American Psychologist* 54, no. 10 (1999): 821–27.

Diener, E., J. Horwitz, and R. A. Emmons. "Happiness of the Very Wealthy." *Social Indicators Research* 16 (1985): 263–74.

Diener, E., and M. E. P. Seligman. "Beyond Money: Toward an Economy of Well-Being." *Psychological Science in the Public Interest* 5, no. 1 (July 2004): 1–31.

Diener, E., E. Sandvik, L. Seidlitz, et al. "The Relationship Between Income and Subjective Well-Being: Relative or Absolute?" *Social Indicators Research* 28 (1993): 195–223.

Ehrenreich, B. *Nickel and Dimed: On (Not) Getting By in America.* New York: Owl Books, 2002.

Helliwell, J. F. "How's Life? Combining Individual and National Variables to Explain Subjective Well-Being." *Economic Modeling* 20 (2003): 331–60.

Jackson, L. A. "Relative Deprivation and the Gender Gap." *Journal of Social Issues* 45, no. 4 (1989): 117–33.

Loscocco, K. A., and G. Spitze. "The Organizational Context of Women's and Men's Pay Satisfaction." *Social Science Quarterly* 72, no. 1 (1991).

Myers, D. G. "The Funds, Friends, and Faith of Happy People." *American Psychologist* 55, no. 1 (2000): 56–67.

Neumark, D., and A. Postlewaite. "Relative Income Concerns and the Rise in Married Women's Employment." *Journal of Public Economics* 70 (1998): 157–83.

Schyns, P. *Income and Life Satisfaction: A Cross-National and Longitudinal Study*. Delft, the Netherlands: Eburon, 2003.

Smith, D. M., K. M. Langa, M. U. Kabeto, et al. "Health, Wealth, and Happiness: Financial Resources Buffer Subjective Well-Being After the Onset of a Disability." *Psychological Science* (In Press).

Veenhoven, R. "Is Happiness Relative?" *Social Indicators Research* 24 (1991): 1–34.

Chapter 9: Reassessing Goals in the Face of Adversity

Brunstein, J. C. "Personal Goals and Subjective Well-Being: A Longitudinal Study." *Journal of Personality & Social Psychology* 65, no. 5 (1993): 1061–70.

Camus, A., and J. O'Brien. *The Myth of Sisyphus*. Eastbourne, England: Gardeners Books, 2000.

Crowe, E., and E. T. Higgins. "Regulatory Focus and Strategic Inclinations: Promotion and Prevention in Decision-Making." *Organizational Behavior and Human Decision Processes* 69, no. 2 (1997): 117–32.

Higgins, E. T. "Beyond Pleasure and Pain." *American Psychologist* 52, no. 12 (1997): 1280–1300.

Higgins, E. T., C. J. Roney, E. Crowe, et al. "Ideal Versus Ought Predilections for Approach and Avoidance: Distinct Self-Regulatory Systems." *Journal of Personality & Social Psychology* 66, no. 2 (1994): 276–86.

Higgins, E. T., J. Shah, and R. Friedman. "Emotional Responses to Goal Attainment: Strength of Regulatory Focus as Moderator." *Journal of Personality & Social Psychology* 72, no. 3 (1997): 515–25.

Kubler-Ross, E. *On Death and Dying*. New York: Simon & Schuster, 1969.

Lampic, C., E. Thurfjell, J. Bergh, et al. "Life Values Before Versus After a Breast Cancer Diagnosis." *Research in Nursing & Health* 25, no. 2 (2002): 89–98.

Lawton, M. P., M. S. Moss, and L. Winter. "Motivation in Later Life: Personal Projects and Well-Being." *Psychology and Aging* 17, no. 4 (2002): 539–47.

Lepore, S. J., and D. T. Eton. "Response Shifts in Prostate Cancer Patients: An Evaluation of Suppressor and Buffer Modes." In *Adaptation to Changing Health: Response Shift in Quality-of-Life Research, 1st ed.*, edited by C. E. Schwartz and M. A. Sprangers, 37–51. Washington, DC: American Psychological Association, 2000.

McNeil, B. J., S. G. Pauker, H. C. Sox, Jr., et al. "On the Elicitation of Preferences for Alternative Therapies." *New England Journal of Medicine* 306, no. 21 (1982): 1259–62.

Sheldon K. M., and L. Houser-Marko. "Self-Concordance, Goal Attainment, and the Pursuit of Happiness: Can There Be an Upward Spiral?" *Journal of Personality & Social Psychology* 80, no. 1 (2001): 152–65.

Ubel, P. A. *Pricing Life: Why It's Time for Health Care Rationing.* Cambridge, MA: MIT Press, 2000.

Updegraff, J. A., S. L. Gable, and S. E. Taylor. "What Makes Experiences Satisfying? The Interaction of Approach-Avoidance Motivations and Emotions in Well-Being." *Journal of Personality & Social Psychology* 86, no. 3 (2004): 496–504.

Chapter 10: Religious Beliefs and Spirituality During Times of Adversity

Argyle, M. "Causes and Correlates of Happiness." In *Well-Being: The Foundations of Hedonic Psychology* edited by D. Kahneman, E. Diener, and N. Schwarz, 213–29. New York: Russell Sage Foundation, 1999.

Beit-Hallahmi, B., and M. Argyle. *The Psychology of Religious Behavior, Belief, and Experience.* London: Routledge and Kegan Paul Press, 1997.

Ellison, C. G. "Religious Involvement and Subjective Well-Being." *Journal of Health & Social Behavior* 32 (1991): 80–99.

Harlow, R. E., and N. Cantor. "Still Participating After All These Years: A Study of Life Task Participation in Later Life." *Journal of Personality & Social Psychology* 71, no. 6 (1996): 1235–49.

Idler, E. L. "Religion, Disability, Depression, and the Timing of Death." *American Journal of Sociology* 97, no. 4 (1992): 1052–79.

McIntosh, D. N., R. C. Silver, and C. B. Wortman. "Religion's Role in Adjustment to a Negative Life Event: Coping with the Loss of a Child." *Journal of Personality & Social Psychology* 65, no. 4 (1993): 812–21.

Myers, D. G. "The Funds, Friends, and Faith of Happy People." *American Psychologist* 55, no. 1 (2000): 56–67.

Pahnke, W. H. "Drugs and Mysticism." *International Journal of Parapsychology* 8 (1966): 295–314.

Pargament, K. "The Bitter and the Sweet: An Evaluation of the Costs and Benefits of Religiousness." *Psychological Inquiry* 13, no. 3 (2002): 168–81.

Pollner, M. "Divine Relations, Social Relations, and Well-Being." *Journal of Health & Social Behavior* 30 (1989): 92–104.

Tix, A. P., and P. A. Frazier. "The Use of Religious Coping During Stressful Life Events: Main Effects, Moderation, and Mediation." *Journal of Consulting & Clinical Psychology* 66, no. 2 (1998): 411–22.

VandeCreek, L., K. Pargament, T. Belavich, et al. "The Unique Benefits of Religious Support During Cardiac Bypass Surgery." *The Journal of Pastoral Care* 53, no. 1 (1995): 19–29.

Chapter 11: Thinking Your Way to Happiness: It's All a Matter of Interpretation

Gable, S. L., H. T. Reis, E. A. Impett, et al. "What Do You Do When Things Go Right? The Intrapersonal and Interpersonal Benefits of Sharing Positive Events." *Journal of Personality & Social Psychology* 87, no. 2 (2004): 228–45.

King, L. A. "The Health Benefits of Writing About Life Goals." *Personality and Social Psychology Bulletin* 27, no. 7 (2001): 798–807.

Langston, C. A. "Capitalizing on and Coping with Daily-Life Events: Expressive Responses to Positive Events." *Journal of Personality & Social Psychology* 67, no. 6 (1994): 1112–25.

Proust, M. "Reply to Une petite question: Et si le monde allait finir . . . Que feriez-vous?" *L'Intransigeant* (14 Aug 1922).

Schwarz, N., and F. Strack. "Evaluating One's Life: A Judgment Model of Subjective Well-Being." In *Subjective Well-Being, 1st ed.*, edited by F. Strack, M. Argyle, and N. Schwarz, 27–47. Oxford: Pergamon Press, 1991.

Index

About the Author

Peter A. Ubel, M.D., is professor of medicine and psychology at the University of Michigan and director of the Center for Behavioral and Decision Sciences in Medicine at the University of Michigan. Trained in internal medicine at the Mayo Clinic, he currently practices primary care, part time, at the Ann Arbor Veterans Affairs Medical Center. His research explores controversial issues about the role of values and preferences in health care decision making, from decisions at the bedside to policy decisions.

Dr. Ubel has won many research awards, including a Presidential Early Career Award for Scientists and Engineers from President Clinton in 2000. He has written more than one hundred scientific articles, published in leading journals such as the *New England Journal of Medicine* and *JAMA,* and has written about health care in publications such as the *New York Times.* He is author of *Pricing Life: Why It Is Time for Health Care Rationing* (MIT Press, 2000). He is an avid tennis player, a classical pianist, and spends innumerable hours wrestling with his two young boys.